THE NEW VEGETARIANS

Books by Rynn Berry

THE VEGETARIANS
THE NEW VEGETARIANS
FAMOUS VEGETARIANS AND
    THEIR FAVORITE RECIPES

THE NEW VEGETARIANS

RYNN BERRY

**PYTHAGOREAN
PUBLISHERS**

NEW YORK   LOS ANGELES

PHOTOGRAPHIC CREDITS
Cloris Leachman ©1993, Walt Disney Productions
Malcolm Muggeridge ©1993, Jill Krementz
Brigid Brophy ©1993, Jill Krementz
Isaac Bashevis Snger ©1993, Nancy Crampton
Dr. Alan Long ©1993, Christopher Francis
Scott and Helen Nearing ©1993, Carole Getzoff
Rynn Berry ©1993, Nancy Crampton
Dick Gregory ©1993, Carmen de Jesus
Bill & Akiko Shurtleff ©1993, Janet Fries

Originally published under the title
"The Vegetarians," by The Autumn Press, Inc.
Brookline, MA 02146.

Revised edition under the new title
published by The Town House Press, Inc.,
Chestnut Ridge, NY 10977.

This revised edition published by
Pythagorean Publishers
P.O. Box 8174
JAF Station
New York, N.Y. 10116.

Cover design by Richard Spencer
Book design and typography by Beverly Stiskin

For information or correspondence please contact the author via the publisher:
PYTHAGOREAN PUBLISHERS
P.O. Box 8174
JAF Station
New York, N.Y. 10116.

This book is printed on durable acid-free paper.

Dedicated to the memory of Helen Howell Moorhead,

my beloved grandmother,

for her love, vision, and generosity.

Table of Contents

Acknowledgments

Many people played a part in bringing this book to fruition. Special thanks are due to Wendy Lipkind for her assistance and moral support beyond the call of duty; to Bill and Ann Tara for allowing me to lodge with them at the East-West Institute during my stay in London; and to Jill Krementz for allowing the use of her photographs of Malcolm Muggeridge, Isaac Bashevis Singer, and Brigid Brophy.

The limitations of space prohibit a detailed description of their various contributions, but I would like to thank John DeSimio, Lauretta Feldman, Brent Greene, Lillian Gregory, Skip Heinecke, Cheryl Lindner, Michael Maslansky, Dvorah Menashe, Anne Moorhead, Kitty Muggeridge, *New Age* magazine, *Parabola*, Ruth Samot, Shanthi, Mo Siegel, Joel Stern, The Vegetarian Society of the United Kingdom, John and Julie Wilcox, and Leo Wilking.

I am especially grateful to my first publisher, Nahum Stiskin, for his faith and encouragement; and I thank Beverly Stiskin for the design and typography of the book, and Shirley Corvo, Susan Willis, and Deborah Balmuth for their enthusiasm and assiduity.

Over the years, F. M. Esfandiary has given me advice and encouragement for which I take this opportunity to thank him.

I would also like to thank my good friend Hideko Abe for her constant encouragement.

Preface

M eat-eating is going out of fashion: the signs and portents are everywhere. At schools and colleges across the country, many of western society's future leaders are converting to vegetarianism. Intellectuals, writers, artists, scholars, actors, famous athletes, social arbiters, and aristocrats are no longer eating the flesh of animals.

Vegetarianism is becoming chic and fashionable, but does this mean that it is only a fashion, an emphemeral fad, and that within the next twenty years it will again become the custom to eat meat? I think it unlikely. Fashions in diet are more tenacious than fashions in clothes and are longer in taking hold. In the world of *haute cuisine,* several hundred years may be the equivalent of ten or twenty in the world of *haute couture.* For example, iced drinks were considered a fad in the Roman Empire; the New World vegetables—such as the potato and tomato—were not admitted into western cooking until two hundred years after they had been imported to Europe as botanical curios in the sixteenth century. In western culture, Greek philosophers such as Empedocles and Pythagoras were perhaps our earliest and most vociferous vegetarians, thus, one hardly could look upon the vegetarian movement as springing full-blown from the head of George Bernard Shaw. In actuality, this fashion in food has taken about twenty-five hundred years to take root.

It is my belief that meat-eating is a fad that was created by Europe's warrior aristocracies. From antiquity until a hundred years or so ago, only the monied classes had the requisite leisure and treasure to either hunt animals or to hire proxies to slaughter animals for their table. Like most aristocratic conventions, flesh-eating was eventually imitated by the other classes whenever possible, not because meat was wholesome or invigorating, but because those higher up the economic scale were eating it. While the diet of kings and nobles included roast venison, beef, rabbit, boar, and quail, the well-to-do families in prosperous, seventeenth century Holland, for instance, could afford meat no more than once a week, and laborers were lucky to get it once a month. Even in mid-nineteenth century France, the home of *haute cuisine,* the lower classes seldom tasted meat more than once a week.

It was much the same throughout northern Europe, as J.C. Furnas observed in *The Americans:*

> The upper classes of post-medieval Northern Europe, particularly in England, got a good deal of meat and fish. But the English lower orders lived largely on bread supplemented by cheese and root vegetables; the Scots chiefly on oatmeal and occasional milk; the Scotch-Irish on potatoes and milk.[1]

The advertised abundance of meat actually provided an incentive for immigration to America. But the results of the democratization of meat-eating in the New World during the past century are cataloged by Gerald Carson:

> The Scotch who flowed into Philadelphia, the Irish "b'hoys" who built the canals and railroads, and all the immigrant arrivals representing other national strains, joined with the

1. (New York: Putnam, 1969) p. 175.

resident American farmer in the ingestion of a God's plenty of food, eating for the first time above a ton of foodstuffs per person per year, with heavy emphasis upon meats. In our rugged democracy all classes could for the first time acquire the palpitations, nightmares, obesity, and eructations formerly the exclusive perquisites of the higher orders of society. Those who could afford it took the waters at Saratoga or Ballston Spa, or turned to a convalescent home for a discipline of compulsory fasting and internal bathing. Those with limited funds could try the extract of colocynth and aloes, or dine penitently when *in extremis* on oatmeal gruel.[2]

Today, the average western laborer can dine as sumptuously as the medieval nobility but this is clearly a mixed blessing, for just as the diets of the aristocracy have become commonplace, so have the royal diseases. Gout, obesity, heart disease, and cancer, which used to haunt the royal families of Europe, have become as common among middle-class America and Europe as they once were rare.

Are these the results of eating animal flesh? Many vegetarian converts seem to think so, as the interviews in this book make plain. Government studies have shown that Seventh-Day Adventists, whose religion forbids meat-eating, have dramatically lower incidences of the diseases that plague meat-eaters. Were more studies of this nature conducted among other vegetarian groups, the findings would likely be the same.

If the flesh diet was palpably lethal, everyone would avoid it. But because meat is, as I believe, a slow-acting poison, people attribute the symptoms it causes to other factors. If they would but lower their gaze, more people might realize that the source of much of their mental and physical ills lies under their very noses—on their dinner plates.

This book is offered in the hope that it will make a constructive contribution to the changing dietary patterns of America and the West. The author believes that such changes are much needed and would benefit our society and its members in this generation—and for generations to come.

---

2. *The Cornflake Crusade* (New York: Rinehart, 1957) p. 30.

Cloris Leachman

C loris Leachman calls it "not noticing the hippopotamus' head among the faces in the room"—the tendency of people to avert their eyes and render invisible what they would find distasteful. Hans Christian Anderson pointed to the same human foible in his fable "The Emperor's New Clothes." Had Leachman been in the crowd when the naked emperor passed through the streets, she would have been the first to break the conspiracy of silence and announce that the king wore no clothes. Certainly, she has done her best to shatter the conspiracy of silence that surrounds the killing of animals for food. On TV talk shows, on the lecture platform and in the press, she rarely misses an opportunity to point out that a meat diet is as morally and nutritionally denuded as the fabled emperor's bottom.

15

Leachman has the courage to stand up for her convictions and her outspokenness has been rewarded by accolades from both animal-protection and nutritional societies.

Born in Des Moines, Iowa on April 30, 1926, she is the eldest child of a Des Moines lumber dealer, Buck Leachman, and a mother, whom she once affectionately referred to as "Jean Kerr in the country." From her mother, Leachman inherited her first name, her irreverent sense of humor, and the belief that she could achieve anything to which she set her mind. He mother saw to it that Leachman had piano lessons from the time she was seven. And although they couldn't afford a piano, Leachman practised her lessons every day on a cardboard keyboard. Later on, her diligence at the keyboard paid off: in September, 1946, as Miss Chicago, she combined beauty with a virtuoso display of dramatic and pianistic talent to win a $1,000 scholarship as one of four finalists in the 1946 Miss America Contest (finalists were unranked in those days). With the scholarship money, she paid for piano and voice lessons in New York and was chosen by Elia Kazan to study in the original group that formed the Actor's Studio.

Within three months of her arrival in New York—after having barely missed being cast in the lead role of the play—Leachman under-studied Nina Foch in *John Loves Mary*. Next she appeared with Shirley Booth in *Come Back Little Sheba*. Then she played Celia in *As You Like It*, with Katherine Hepburn, and was vividly remembered twelve years later by critic Harriet Van Horne as "the loveliest Celia imaginable." Shortly thereafter, she was asked by Rodgers and Hammerstein to play the role of Nellie Forbush in the original cast production of *South Pacific* for a limited engagement on Broadway.

Leachman withdrew from a blossoming Broadway career in the mid–1950s to raise five children with her producer husband George Englund. But she remained active in films and most recently television. She is probably most familiar to the public as TV's "Phyllis" and as the comic villainess in Mel Brooks' films *Young Frankenstein* and *High Anxiety*. Other films in which her portrayal of a character has often transcended the film itself include *Kiss Me Deadly, The Chapman Report, Butch Cassidy and The Sundance Kid, Lovers and Other Strangers, WUSA, Daisy Miller,* and *North Avenue Irregulars*. In 1972 she received the Academy Award for her brilliant performance in *The Last Picture Show,* and in the years since, she has been awarded the Golden Globe and four Emmys for her dramatic roles on television.

I've read that you had a revelation while you were rinsing a chicken under the faucet: it suddenly occurred to you that what you were doing wasn't very different from bathing a baby.

I had a new born baby, and it was exactly the same experience, yes—except that the chicken's tail, or as we used to say in Iowa "the Pope's nose," comes to a point.

Is this what prompted you to become a vegetarian?

No, no. I had gotten very ill with asthma suddenly, and I'd never had it before during my childhood or even during my adult years. And I know that it's a syndrome; it isn't just one thing. However, I know if you remove one piece of the pie, one symptom of the syndrome, that you can probably alleviate it. In fact they are finding out new things all the time that have an effect on it: from herbs to acupuncture, to fasting—which worked in my case—to change of geography, to getting rid of all the animals—feathers and fur and so forth—dust, to getting rid of the emotional strife and stress—all those things. And Harvard did a study which said that at the bottom of asthma, the very bottom, is "fear of desertion by the mother." I think that was operating in my case, because my husband and I had been separated for a year, and I knew when I met him that it was just like putting my mother and my father and Saint George himself all into one basket.

So I'm sure all of those things were operating. However, *fasting* alone really cured me, which meant for me, fresh-squeezed orange juice drunk instantly alternated with water one day, and the next day fresh-squeezed grapefruit juice alternated with water. The next day I had ripe watermelon all one day; and the next day I had orange juice alternated with water again, always fresh-squeezed, drunk instantly, so that the vitamins aren't destroyed by the light. And that did it for me. I did it for ten days. By the fourth day, the appetite control in your brain—the appestat—turns off so that you are no longer experiencing hunger. And not only that, but a great feeling of energy and euphoria washes over you, and during this time, everything that's ever been wrong with me was cured: the asthma, the hayfever, the arthritis in my fingers, the sleeplessness. There was no suffering at all; it's not like being deprived as when one is on a diet.

Is this when you lost your desire for meat?

Then I began reading a lot of books from the health food store. One of them was *Fasting Can Save Your Life* by Dr. Shelton; another was *Rational Fasting* by Arnold Ehret. *Raw Vegetable Juices* by Walker is another. A book that is must reading is *Sugar Blues* by Gloria Swanson's husband, William Dufty, as is Dr. Paavo Airola's *How To Get Well*. All these books are very good to read for cross-references. Another was *Raw Salads*. I just started to read, and I began to find out what is wrong with meat. We'll never hear that from the meat industry, incidentally. That's a very powerful lobby in Washington as is the dairy industry.

Money is at the root of it all—what's making money for people. Power begets power and where the money is there's more power and that begets more power and pretty soon all of those people are in control. They're controlling everybody including our schools, because you'll never hear about vegetarianism in school. They will teach you only about the four basic food groups—which is erroneous. In my opinion, drinking cow's milk causes as much tooth decay as eating sweets ever did, but you'll never hear that discussed in school.

I used to love cheese, but I seldom eat it now. If I want some I'll grate just a little on the top of a salad. I don't drink milk any more. After the age of two, you don't need cow's milk. Of course you need calcium, but there are so many better ways to get it.

The Israelites had a prohibition against seething a calf in its mother's milk. If you think about it, it really is barbaric to eat hamburger or veal, and wash it down with a glass of milk that may be from its own mother.

Oh my God, yes! There are so many people who don't even know what we're talking about and all they're left with is even more guilt.

Do you owe any of your success as an actress to your diet?

The fact that I don't get sick, and can work extraordinary hours, and have enormous stamina what with caring for five children at home. I'm not toxic and tired and exhausted from eating food that holds me down. My diet supports me; it's a life support system that I have.

Now I have condensed my ideas into a few simple rules of thumb. I just spoke at the National Health Organization which convened in Pasadena for the last three days this past weekend. They gave me an award for setting an example of vibrant health to the nation.

Anyway, here are some of the things that I told them. What makes sense to me is that your food should come from as close to the tree or the ground as you can get it. Generally, don't eat anything brown or white; and only eat foods that are colorful: purple, red, orange, yellow, green—a vibrant artist's palette, so that they picture for you and your own palate something mouthwatering. The only exceptions would be brown rice, grains, potatoes with the skins on.

Why do you eliminate foods that are white and brown?

I don't eliminate them; I just don't choose them. Meat, dairy products, candy, drugs, alcohol, vegetables, every food-stuff that you could imagine, if they are all arrayed in front of me, I would choose what is colorful, what is alive, what is beautiful, what is healthy. Do you see the difference? It's not that I eliminate certain foods. I don't even *see* them because I choose only what appeals to my senses: my intelligence, my eyes, my nose, my tactile sense, my sense of taste—all of them.

And I reject the whole vocabulary that has arisen around doctor talk, such as "diet", "regime", "are you allowed?" "can you have?" There's guilt if you cheat, and there's deprivation if you diet. It's a never-ending, vicious circle of defeat and sorrow, and nobody loses weight.

You see, I don't want to be a big bore on this subject and become so rigid that I separate myself from the very people with whom I share life's experiences. That's why I've been so appalled and outraged at the sufferings of untold millions, and the amount of money into the billions that is spent on promoting this dieting mentality. I reject the whole thing and I know it is totally unnecessary!

You've arrived at your wisdom through trial and error.

Yes, through experience. But more than that, my experience was corroborated by what I read after I'd had the experience. There are people who say, "Well, if you believe it's good for you, then it becomes good for you, through belief." But none of those people who maintains that health is an act of faith or a belief system has any knowledge of what fasting is.

For example, this so-called grapefruit fast is not a fast at all, in fact. The grapefruit fast, as it's promoted by Dr. Whoever-It-Is, is essentially a meat diet. You just eat grapefruit before you eat everything else.

Grapefruit actually does start a fat-burning process, but to call this a fast is a distortion; it's short-lived, short-term. The "dieting" mentality leads to unhappy experiences; I'm interested in an approach to eating that is a way of life, where the road just unfolds before you and leads you into good feelings and uplifting experiences.

Why do you suppose doctors don't advocate vegetarianism?

They don't know anything about it. They don't study it. They're ignorant. In other words, doctors study diseases and drugs. I study health, feeling terrific, and looking vital and alive.

The natural way is so much easier and guilt-free. For example, some people would rather give the appearance of feeling well by having a face-lift, exercising violently, or dieting severely—but they don't solve the problem; they only disguise it. If they ate properly, they wouldn't have to strain to *seem* fit; they would *be* fit. The simplest and most natural way usually turns out to be the easiest. Consider nursing, for instance. It's obviously the most natural way to nourish a baby, but it's also the easiest; you don't have to wake up in the middle of the night and fix bottles. If you're a vegetarian, you don't have to cook food in a smelly, greasy kitchen, or clean a lot of pots and pans with the rancid grease on them. Ugh! Though it may seem easier to take a slab of dead flesh and toss it in a broiler, it's much more interesting to do something creative with vegetables.

So that my children don't have to snack on sweets or bowls of cereal—it's no better than sawdust, you know—I set out platters of avocadoes, pineapples, papayas, bananas, almonds, dried figs and prunes. Instead of coffee, I serve delicious, steaming herb teas from Celestial Seasonings; I serve organic apple juice in place of milk. I have the most beautiful golden honey for the herb tea—and so, you see, no one need feel deprived on a vegetarian diet.

Or, instead of a piece of dead flesh in the middle of the plate, I'll put a baked yam, or a baked potato. You just scrub it, and put it in the oven at 500 degrees. Don't use foil or anything, because the minerals are right under the skin. You bake it until it's absolute crunch—about 1½ hours. You don't want to scorch it. After that, you cut it open immediately, or it gets soft from the steam inside. If it does go soft, just pop it back in the oven at 500 degrees until it gets crunchy again. Sometimes I coat it with a little oil so it won't be dry. Then I put a soft avocado on the table, and you just spread the avocado on the potato like butter. On top of that goes a layer of alfalfa sprouts with a little lemon-and-oil dressing seasoned with Vege-Sal instead of salt. And it is fantastic!

Green peas—not Chinese snow peas, but regular, garden-variety peas—you can steam in the pods for just five minutes. Don't let them become soft. They should be almost raw, but steaming hot. Then just put them in the middle of the table in a big bowl. Insert one end of the pod in your mouth, pull with your teeth, and the peas pop right up at the other end. Well, I mean, look how colorful it is! It's an experience! It's fun! And the kids love to eat them that way!

I've stopped cutting the ends off greenbeans. Why should you have to stand at the kitchen sink and fritter away your time chopping, shredding, or nipping beans? Just wash them and throw them in the top of a steamer; it couldn't be quicker. Then what I do is to take the end of each string bean and join them together to form a loop, and then eat the loop. It's great fun. I love to eat with my fingers anyway.

If you don't use your fingers, I think you're missing some of the experience of eating.

Of course you are convinced that a mother should nurse her own baby.

Unquestionably; I came upon an article that had appeared in an issue of *Life* some years back, in which they published the results of many studies showing that, strange as it may seem, the baby's brain develops more evenly when it's nursed, because when you nurse a baby, you change sides. That was some years ago, but you don't hear too much about these things nowadays because the formula companies do everything they can to discourage nursing—in a very underhanded way, incidentally—not frontally, but by innuendo and insinuation. They try to spread the rumor that mother's milk is not good for babies any more because of all the pollutants we breathe, all the additives, traces of radioactive fallout, and pesticides that we absorb in our food.

But this is true only in the most isolated cases, if at all. A breast-fed baby as opposed to a bottle-fed baby always smells sweet. It gets much more fondling and holding from its mother; a baby can't prop up a bottle. Breast-feeding connects the mother and the baby in a way that they can never be connected later. When you nurse a baby, there's actually a hormone that's released through the lactation that makes the mother calm and dozy.

When you don't complete that trinity of having a baby, you are cheating yourself as well as the baby. Pregnancy is the first part of the trinity; birth is the second; and nursing the baby is the third. Many women develop what are called the post-partum blues. I've known some women who've had severe and prolonged depressions because they didn't complete the trinity.

Most doctors and most women have the misconception that three months is a good time to end nursing. What they don't realize is that after three months it really gets easy; you can nurse a baby just once a day. You don't need to feed a baby any solid food at all until it is six months old. In fact, you shouldn't; you're only cheating the baby out of the best nutrition possible.

On the other hand, it's undeniable that many mothers are not properly nourished. In that case I would have to concede that it would be better for these women to bottle-feed their babies.

Do you think that vegetarian mothers give a more nourishing milk?

Exactly. Also, I don't think mothers should feed their babies canned baby foods.

Did you prepare your own baby foods!?

No, I didn't; but now that I've learned, I can see what pap these commercial baby foods are. A baby who is fed fruits and vegetables prepared by its mother will actually have a healthier flesh tone. You can tell from looking at people's flesh what kind of food they are eating.

Do you think meat today is a status symbol?

Oh very much. Yes, it certainly is. It's practically mandatory to serve steak or roast beef at charity affairs because people feel they're not getting their money's worth if they're not served a fancy cut of meat. Poorer people also feel that if they can have a steak on the table that this is a symbol of prosperity, because they have been indoctrinated to believe this by our culture and by the meat industry.

What happens when your're invited to an elegant Beverly Hills dinner party and the guests are dining on Beef Wellington or Rack of Lamb? Do you mind inconveniencing your hosts?

I never have occasion to do that. Anytime I attend some elegant dinner, there's plenty of food to eat. And people are always more than willing to give me their vegetables.

But I don't often go to very elegant Beverly Hills dinner parties. I can't remember when I've been to one. I'm busy with my own home and family, and that's where my interest lies. I'd much rather go out for dinner to a restaurant with my family or friends than go to some big dinner party anyway, and that's what I tend to do.

And anybody who comes to my home seems to be delighted with the food I serve. I think we eat better than kings and queens. The food is so colorful, delicious, fresh, and varied. People say, "Don't you ever miss a piece of juicy charcoal-broiled steak?" And I say, "No, I didn't choose that. I chose a beautiful yam, a fresh-green spinach salad seasoned with a little garlic, some olive oil and lemon, with a little Vege-Sal on it. My God, that's tasty!"

In television and movie dramas, there seems to be very little emphasis on eating.

Most good actors frequently are eating, if you'll notice. In one scene or another, the best actors are usually eating, biting or chewing something. Especially if you don't have a very well-written scene, you get something going around your mouth. It's a much-used device that always works. But, it depends on the nature of the film; if it's a medical film, or a medical series, you don't see people eating too much, because they're being operated on.

Also, I've noticed that in movies, warriors and cowboys never seem to be eating.

No, but they drink a lot of black coffee, all of those people. Coffee has been a big device. It used to be cigarettes; now they're reduced to just coffee.

I don't even buy coffee any more. In my house I serve a delicious steaming herb tea from Celestial Seasonings, and my guests are just as pleased to have it; it's very full-bodied.

Supposing a script called for you to eat some sort of meat. Would you do it?

No, I would either change the script or substitute something. I've always substituted things.

Cloris Leachman 23

Do you mean, in the past, scripts have asked you to eat foods that you found objectionable?

Well, usually it isn't that specific; or if it is, it usually isn't that important. Frequently the script will specify white bread, and I will always ask for brown bread. Instead of lunch-meat, I'll ask for avocado or cucumber sandwiches; if I can't get those I'll eat peanut butter.

Do you consider yourself an ethical vegetarian?

Well, I'm a realist. As soon as I realized that I didn't need meat to survive or to be in good health, I began to see how forlorn it all is. If only we had a different mentality about the drama of the cowboy and the range and all the rest of it. It's a very romantic notion, an entrenched part of American culture, but I've seen, for example, pigs waiting to be slaughtered, and their hysteria and panic was something I shall never forget for the rest of my life. And the crowding—the way they were penned up without being allowed to move, much less exercise.

Do you think we shall see the emancipation of animals within our lifetime?

No, never. The powers that be—the government and the money interests—won't give it up; it's too profitable. Take vivisection, for example: Animal experimentation is a $4 billion a year industry in our country alone. Now the emerging nations are being encouraged to supply laboratories in the United States with animals that will ultimately be tortured in ridiculous experiments. And universities are being funded in large measure by these vivisection laboratories, staffed by so-called scientists who are getting their salaries paid by foundations and charities whose funding comes from public contributions.

Under the name of "research" more butchery and torture of animals is committed. I've studied this at great length, and I've found that only 5 percent of it provides any new research data; 95 percent of the experimental data could be obtained from computers. Much of it is redundant and duplicates experiments that have already been done, going back to the 1500s. If you change one detail of an experiment, you will be funded by Congress all over again.

The Congress is voting millions of dollars for this, because it brings money into their states. So it's very, very powerful and gigantic. It interlocks with **big government** and **big business**; its tentacles extend into the governments and economies of countries all over the world. The traffic in laboratory animals is extremely profitable. There are huge sums to be made from the breeding and transporting of animals for the laboratories in the universities. The irony of it is that much of the money for the needless torture of animals comes from people who know nothing about the vivisection that goes on in the labs, but who donate money for purposes of research.

Doesn't the fact that more people are becoming vegetarian hold out some hope that we may see the end of vivisection in our lifetime?

Yes, slightly. But you have no idea of the extent of public ignorance on this subject; it is abysmal. I have boxes of material documenting the cruelty involved in these animal experiments. No one can read it and ever have pleasant dreams again. It's available to everyone through the animal protection societies, but most people are not interested. They want to do what is comfortable and familiar, and routine, especially with regard to eating. People eat not only to fill their stomachs, but also to repeat a comforting ritual.

Do you think that diets are sexually stereotyped? That is, do you think a flesh diet is traditionally regarded as being more masculine, and a vegetable diet more feminine?

Oh definitely! More wives have killed their husbands! Do you know how many widows there are in this country compared to widowers? The disporportion is staggering. Most women have killed their husbands by feeding them meat. "Oh my husband is a 'meat and potatoes man' you know," and even if they don't eat much meat, they feed it to their husbands.

A woman's lunch generally consists of what?

They're usually on a diet, so I would say a salad.

And a businessman's lunch?

Steak. Meat and potatoes.

Do you think that with the dissolution of sexual stereotypes, this will incline more people to eat vegetarian food?

It may; it may have a definite effect. Lots of people are opening up to good things these days.

Do you think that as more and more people become vegetarian, it will usher in a new Golden Age?

I don't know, there will always be some asshole who didn't get the word.

Aren't the people beginning to get the word?

Not if Washington can help it.

You're not optimistic then.

Well, I am amazed at the proliferation of these ideas; it's very exciting. Also, I think people are becoming fed-up with the bedside manner, doctor-talk, medical propaganda, hospitals, and operations; they're looking for alternatives.

I'll tell you something: one of the most shocking things I have ever seen was an advertisement in I. Magnin's for a prosthetic bra, designed specially for women who've had mastectomies. "Come to our department and be fitted following your mastectomy." It's become so commonplace that a prosthetic bra is considered high fashion and is advertised as such by chic department stores. Women are having mastectomies the way kids used to have their tonsils out— automatically. It's become the latest fad operation.

Totally unnecessary. Totally 100,000 percent unnecessary! Doesn't everybody know that? I mean doesn't *everybody* know that?

You mean if they become vegetarians.

Not only that; of course that. The whole way they live their lives. Women who nurse their babies, for example, are must less susceptible to breast cancer. That to me is the epitome of how brainwashed we are.

Ironically, one of the criticisms commonly leveled against the vegetarian diet is that it has a tranquilizing effect upon the system. In our society, a "meat-and-potatoes" diet is thought to be necessary to give people that "fire in the belly" that they need to be successful. How do you feel about that?

They may have more fire in their bellies than vegetarians, but they pay the price. They drop dead prematurely; they're all taking pills to lower their high blood pressure instead of realizing that they wouldn't have high blood pressure if they ate properly.

Meat is formed from the amino acids that the animals derive from the fodder and the grasses that they eat. After taking animal protein—the highly complex, organized tissue that is meat—into their bodies, meat-eaters must break it back down into the amino acids that our bodies can reform back into animal protein, human protein, and in the process, the meat putrefies and toxins are released into the system. You can still tell a meat-eater from looking at one. Their flesh begins to be different. Even with young people, you can tell pretty much what they're eating from looking at their skin.

In order for your system to thrive, ideally, it should be slightly on the alkaline rather than the acid side. If you're acidic, it gives rise to all sorts of problems, from shortness of temper to hysteria, and to breaking down the system and making it a breeding-ground for diseases.

Do you think the prevalent modern diseases are the result of eating meat?

You can't just separate what we eat from our whole way of life. But meat and dairy products are certainly two of the biggest killers.

From your experience, do you think that vegetarians can be just as effective as meat-eaters without endangering their health?

I think they can do anything they want! I think you can be a vegetarian and be tremendously happy and successful and last as long as you want—not as if you were preserved in a bottle and pickled—but truly to have the organs and the outlook of a child or a young person. I do. And I'm very excited by the way these ideas are proliferating.

Vegetarian Cooking Class

presented by
Tori Kamppi, R.N.
of *Natural Radiance,* New York

Date
Sunday, May 3

Time
3:00 to 6:00 PM

Location
111 E. 87th Street
(between Park and Lexington)

Fee: $25.00

Registration Deadline: April 27

Space is limited, so call
212~861~3886 or 800~979~8674
and reserve your spot today!

"Let your food be your medicine and your medicine be your food."
—Hippocrites

Bill Shurtleff

I n 1975 a mysterious white substance called "tofu" started turning up on dinner plates all over America. Because it was high in protein, high in fiber, and low in cholesterol with a remarkable ability to mimic any flavor, it was being touted as the perfect food. Not since (as legend has it) Marco Polo returned from China bearing pasta noodles, had such an important foodstuff arrived from the Orient. So, who was responsible for introducing this marvelous food into Western cuisine? (Actually Japanese and Chinese restaurants had been serving it to their Western customers for years — but always within an exclusively Asian cultural context). For without the intervention of this mysterious benefactor from the East, tofu would never have made the leap from wok to frying pan. Could it have been a Buddhist monk (the original purveyors of tofu in Asia)? Or, maybe a wandering scholar (gypsy scholars had been agents of cultural change in Medieval Europe)? Or perhaps a vegetarian gourmet eager to share his culinary discoveries in the East with the jaded palates of the West?

The short answer is all three of the above. For Bill Shurtleff, who with his Tokyo-born wife Akiko Aoyagi, wrote the *Book of Tofu, The Book of Miso, The Book of Tempeh,* and other books on soyfoods (which made tofu a household name in America), has been by turns a Zen Buddhist monk, a Stanford-educated scholar, and a vegetarian chef, who plied his skills in the kitchen of the Zen monastery at Tassajara.

The son of a wealthy California construction company owner and a housewife, Shurtleff graduated from Stanford in 1963 with honors in humanities, physics, and engineering. He seemed destined for a career as an engineer or physicist, but like so many of the young men who came of age in the late 1960s, he took some unconventional turns on his way to becoming the maestro of tofu. Much to the dismay of his parents, he threw up a promising career to become a cook at the Tassajara Zen Mountain Center. He then traveled to Japan to train as a Zen monk, married a vivacious Japanese fashion designer, wrote a best-selling book on tofu, and ended by becoming a conduit for introducing the health-giving foods of the Orient to the West.

In the mid 1970s Bill and Akiko left Japan to settle in Lafayette, California where they founded the Soyfoods Center, and set up as consultants to a burgeoning soyfoods industry that they played such a vital part in developing.

How long have you been a vegetarian?

Since 1966.

What prompted you to become a vegetarian?

I was a student at Stanford University, living in a community with about fifteen other people. This was during the Vietnam War, and a number of people in that community, including myself, were doing yoga, and meditation, and all of us were doing draft resistance. A number of people in the community, who took it upon themselves to be the cooks, were vegetarians. Many of the rest of us, who ate the food without really understanding what was happening, gradually realized that we weren't eating any meat, which was fine. We liked the food. We found that the food bill was low, and that was part of the reason for its appeal.

So there was an economic consideration.

There was an economic consideration, although it was never discussed.

So I sort of slid into it. And it wasn't until a year-and-a-half or so after this that I went to a Zen monastery in the mountains of Big Sur, named Tassajara. There, for the first time, I really began to think about the implications of a vegetarian diet.

Was it mandatory that the community members at Tassajara become vegetarians?

Let't put it this way: It's at the end of a thirty-mile road, and all the food that you eat is cooked for you.

Was it Buddhist vegetarian cuisine?

Yes, it's Buddhist vegetarian cuisine, *shojin ryori* in Japanese. So, even if you hadn't wanted to be a vegetarian, that's all that was served. But by this time, I had embraced the diet wholeheartedly, and after I had been there for about a year, I became a cook. That required me to learn more about the nutritional aspects of a vegetarian diet, and the more I studied it, the more I liked it.

Is that when you discovered tofu? While you were a cook at Tassajara?

Yes. We would serve tofu once or twice-a-week, usually cubed and put in a soup.

That was your first taste of tofu?

Right.

What was the genesis of your writing The Book of Tofu, *the book that introduced tofu to the West? I know that you were living in Japan as a Buddhist devotee; that you were studying Japanese; and that you were subsisting on twenty-three cents a day, but what was the chain of events that led you to write* The Book of Tofu?

When I went to Japan, I had been living at Tassajara Zen Mountain Center for two-and-a-half years, and basically had no money. So I had to live extremely frugally when I was in Japan, and some money that I expected to come to me, never came. Consequently, I evolved a diet that was basically the same every day. I cooked my own brown rice, and I had one cake of tofu, which was twelve ounces, and cost thirty yen — eight and a half cents. And I usually had a cucumber, and some miso on top of the tofu.

Did you learn how to make this concoction at Tassajara?

More or less. I never learned it, I just figured it out. I knew that I wanted whole grains and a protein source. Cucumber topped it off because cucumbers were very cheap. I just had the same thing every day. Each morning, I would go to the local tofu shop, and pick up a cake of fresh tofu — that was the only way you could get it. The tofu shop was just around the corner from where I lived. At the time, it was one of the 38,000 tofu shops in Japan. So, without thinking much more about it — because I was concentrating on learning Japanese at this time, not on studying tofu, I spent my first year in Japan on that kind of diet. At the end of that year, a number of significant things happened. I met my future wife, Akiko, and my Zen master, Suzuki Roshi, passed away. So my original purpose for being in Japan kind of vanished. Two other events precipitated *The Book of Tofu:* One was a visit to local tofu shop, spending the morning watching the master make tofu. The second event occurred when a Buddhist friend of ours invited us to go to *Sasanoyuki,* which is a famous tofu restaurant in Tokyo. I had never heard of a tofu restaurant before; so when he said, "you ought to come to this place, mostly for the food", we went there; and here was tofu being served in all of these delicious ways, very inexpensively, in a beautiful environment with a waterfall and a big picture window. Because of my long-term interest in food and world hunger, I began to think that this tofu was really something! You know, I hadn't appreciated it fully. I had just taken it for granted. So I put two and two together, and said "tofu is really amazing!" It has been a wonderful food for me at a time when I've had very little money. The making of it is a beautiful art. It can be made into all these delicious dishes. Why don't we write something about it? I was quite sure that there had been nothing written in English on tofu, as I had never seen a book in English on tofu in all my years at Tassajara. So I said to myself: this would be a nice project that would allow me to use the Japanese that I had learned, and to do something worthwhile while I was in Japan. What's more, my wife-to-be, Akiko, was a very good cook; so I said let's write a little book on tofu. One of the things that most Westerners were unaware of was that there were five or six different types of tofu. Until I came to Japan, I had only been aware of one. Here, in Japan there were tofu burgers, and tofu pouches, and grilled tofu, and all these different types. So, we thought we would take a couple of months, and write a little book about it, and get the word out. But one of my biggest problems in life is that when I start something, I have an inexhaustible curiosity, and can't stop until all the questions are answered. So what started as an innocent little venture turned into a mammoth research project. So for three-and-a-half years, we did nothing but write that book.

How did you sustain yourself?

The Universe supports those who are doing things to help other people. I don't say that lightly; I believe that very sincerely. I believe that the Universe always furthers people who are trying to help others. But, at the time I decided to write *The Book of Tofu,* I had virtually no funds, and no source of income at all. Within about a month, we had a publisher for the book, and a researching job.

I notice that you dedicated The Book of Tofu *to your Zen master, Suzuki Roshi.*

Right.

It was really the Zen priests who first brought tofu from China to Japan, was it not?

I think that's probably true. It's not clearly documented; but I wouldn't say Zen — it was Buddhist priests. And it was in the Buddhist temples that it really gained a foothold in Japan. From there, laymen came and learned about it in the restaurants that interfaced between the temple, and/or the monastery and the community. The laymen took it out of the temple, and began to make tofu in small commercial tofu shops; from there it spread to many commercial tofu shops.

I gather that these Buddhist missionaries brought it to Japan in the seventh century A.D., or thereabouts.

The earliest known reference in Japan was in 1183 A.D.

Was that in the Heian period?

Yes, the late Heian.

It seems to me that they placed a greater emphasis on the nonviolent aspects of Buddhism during the Heian period. The taboos against meat-eating were more closely observed than they are today.

The taboos against meat-eating were very strictly observed until 1868 — which was when the Meiji Reformation took place. The prohibition in Japan was against four-leggeds in the society as a whole. Only renegade, counter-culture type people would eat four-leggeds. Japanese people *do* eat fish. And I don't think that they have ever had a feeling that eating a fish was a violent act — as a culture. However, monks did not eat fish. In fact there is a pejorative term for a monk who eats fish. He is called *namagusa bozu,* which means "fishy smelling monk."

Have you ever read Ivan Morris's book The World of the Shining Prince? *It's a reconstruction of social life during the Heian period.*

No, I haven't. You mean the era of Prince Genji?

Yes. Morris points out that the tenets of Buddhism were very firmly held during this period. Hunting was looked down upon by the aristocracy and even warriors were held in contempt. This was before the samurai ethos arose. Of course one of the reasons for the downfall of Heian culture was that the Heian aristocrats were so highly aesthetic and so gentle in their behavior that they were incapable of defending themselves against the provincial warriors who eventually overthrew them. At any rate the Japanese people in Heian times were encouraged to acquire Buddhist merit by treating animals humanely. Special ponds were set aside so that people could free and feed fish and crabs.

I know that has been a practice throughout Japanese history, but it sounds quite reasonable that it would have been stronger during the Heian than it was later.

Even the most self-indulgent aristocrats during this period were largely vegetarian. Whereas the Heian aristocrats' Western counterparts were carnivores, who were. . .

Degenerate and dissolute. And the Japanese aristocrats were among the first Japanese to take up Buddhism, and that may have something to do with it.

Do you think that tofu is a concomitant of Buddhism? Wherever Buddhism has traveled as a religion, it seems to have been accompanied by soyfoods.

Well, I'd say that's true. And I would say that the spread of soyfoods from China to Japan was initiated largely by Buddhists and that the spread of soyfoods to the United States in the recent wave, which has been "the soyfoods movement", had a fairly strong connection with Buddhism.

It's curious how Buddhist religion and tofu are so fatefully intertwined.

Right.

It's not surprising that the arrival of tofu in America has also been accompanied by an upsurge of interest in Buddhism.

Right.

Upstate New York for example is dotted with Buddhist monasteries and retreats. In Rochester, Roshi Philip Kapleau holds forth.

Incidentally, there is a tofu company that has been associated with his Zendo ever since the early days, called Northern Soy.

I know that he has written books, espousing vegetarianism.

Yes, I think they're very good books.

It's curious that Buddhism seems to have provided the impetus for carrying tofu and miso to Japan in the Nara period, as well as to the other countries of Asia. Now again it seems to have provided the impetus for bringing it to America.

Right, it's constantly moving eastward.

Would you say that the soybean has the capacity to liberate man from his meat-centered diet?

It certainly has. The soybean is unequaled in its ability to liberate man from his meat-centered diet. That's the kind of statement I do not consider to be hyperbole.

One thing that I've noted in your books on soyfoods is that the samurai or nobility play a key role in paving the way for the acceptance of these new foods in Japan during the Kamakura period. They substituted tofu for fish in their morning miso soup. In a sense they acted as food tasters as well as taste-makers for the country. They set the tone in diet as well as in dress. And this filters down to the middle and lower classes.

It differed from period to period. I would say that the nobility and the monks were the people who played the greatest role in introducing soyfoods into Japan. They were the pioneers initially. Then the samurai took it up during a later period — the Kamakura period, which started in 1185 A.D. Those would be the three points of entrance.

What attracted the samurai to tofu? Because the Western knight, who was the counterpart of the samurai, was anything but vegetarian. At meals, the medieval knights prided themselves on guzzling as much animal food and alcohol as they could. Whereas the samurai were abstemious, and self-denying, and somewhat Spartan in their tastes.

Very definitely. The samurai as martial artist, which was only one of the roles that samurai played, was in training his whole life. As a practitioner of The Way—many of the samurai were practicing under a living Zen master—the samurai would have had to follow the precepts of Buddhism, which meant no animal products at all. So, it would follow quite logically that they would have a diet similar to monks.

Even though they were professional warriors?

They were and they weren't professional warriors. They were *not* in the sense that the good ones tried not ever to unsheathe the sword. They didn't go around killing people indiscrimately.

In many periods of Japanese history, the samurai was best who could deal with things without violence. Remember they were Buddhists, and Buddhists were basically non-violent. Of course, not all samurai were like that and not all periods were like that.

In the beginning they were more idealistic, I guess.

Yes. I don't know how many samurai movies you've seen, but there is usually a sense that the really good swordsman doesn't often engage in swordplay. He tries to prevail in subtler ways.

Only if provoked does he reach for his sword.

Right.

It's like the storied western gunfighter of many a Hollywood shoot-'em-up.

Sure. The best thing is to be able to hold your hands by your hips, and have the other guy shrink away in fear.

Somewhere you mentioned that the farmers or the peasants had to pay their tribute to the feudal lords in the form of rice. They were left with the broken rice and the barley. So white rice has been associated with the aristocracy.

Oh yes!

Whereas barley has been confounded with the peasantry.

Always. And not only in Japan. In Korea that's true. They have barley only days in Korea. In China, small grains, barley and other things are what's left over.

Also in the West, white sugar, white-floured bread, white meats (such as milk-fed veal), and creamy desserts were prized by the European nobility; whereas the dark, coarse-grained breads, the dark sugars, the unrefined grains, fruits and vegetables were eaten by the European peasantry until the twentieth century.

Very definitely. It's only recently that that trend is starting to be reversed. There has been a long historical trend towards wanting to eat nobility food.

In Japan too, food favored by the nobility seems to be associated with whiteness—for instance the whiteness of refined rice, and mochi cake. Whereas the foods of darker hues—the darker misos like barley miso have been considered a peasant food.

I think that's a fair comparison. The light colored miso might seem a little more refined and aristocratic.

In terms of vegetarianism, the white-colored, over-refined foods in Japan as in the West seem to cluster together. Fiberless foods such as white bread, white rice, white sugar, alcohol, meat—tend to be preferred by the nobility; while the dark-hued, high-fiber foods are favored by the peasantry.

That's right, refined foods, sugar, and meat keep the same company.

There's a rather alarming statistic that I came upon recently—that the consumption of animal protein in Japan had risen thirty-seven percent from 1960 to 1971.

I'm surprised that it's not more than that. I'll bet it *is* more than that. Yes, there has been a steady and accelerating consumption of meat in Japan until 1983 when the Japanese started to become aware of the perils of imitating the Western diet. There is now a backlash. Now there is a definite tendency to return to more traditional Japanese foods. When we were there in 1985 we saw a gigantic growth in the natural foods industry; a lot of interest in organically grown vegetables and a lot of interest in tofu. I could hardly believe how much the image of tofu in Japan had changed between 1976 and 1983. So I think that the beginning of the end of that process is starting in Japan: namely the imitation of the American meat-centered diet.

In America, and increasingly in Europe, it would seem that the intelligentsia are being drawn to a meatless diet.

Yes, I would say that the more intelligent people are drawn to it.

You point out in The Book of Tempeh *that soyfoods have been somewhat lacking in prestige in Malaysia and Japan. Premier Sukarno of Indonesia exhorted the Malaysians not to be a tempeh nation.*

That's changing now, fairly rapidly.

Isn't that because Westerners are now discovering the nutritional benefits of soyfoods and Westerners are setting the culinary trends for Asians?

I think that whenever you have an inexpensive food in a country, a lot of people who don't have much money eat it; and people as they get money aspire to things that are more expensive. So tempeh which is one of the least expensive sources of protein in Indonesia, was widely eaten by poor people, although as we state in our *Book of Tempeh*, it is also widely eaten by all classes of people, and in some way that I don't quite understand, it got a pejorative image. But I heard recently from a number of Indonesian researchers in the Netherlands and in Indonesia, there's been a big shift in its image now; and in fact, Indonesia put on an international tempeh conference last summer that was a big success. Tempeh has been getting a lot of media coverage, and the image is changing, which I'm happy to see. Likewise with tofu in Japan, when I would tell people in Japan that I was studying tofu, and that I was a university graduate, they just couldn't understand it at all.

Paradoxically, young, open-minded Americans seem to be drawn to the tofu- and tempeh-centered diet of pre-war Asian countries, while the diet of the Asian countries has become more meat-centered and westernized. There seems to be a cultural interchange of dietary values at work here, whereby Americans are adopting the soy-food-centered diet of pre-World War II Asia, and the Asians have been adopting the meat-centered diet of the West. It would appear that the Asian countries are looking West for their dietary cues.

That's for sure.

Is that because they associate flesh foods with the might and affluence of the West?

That's a good question. I definitely think that there is that component in it. Particularly after the defeat of Japan in World War II. But it's part of a whole cultural complex that they're taking on. In that sense, when you say "might and power," I think it's in the larger political and international arena that they see America as this superpower—maybe that's the best term—and aspire toward that whole complex of things, and diet is part of it.

But now that Westerners are adopting the formerly low status foods of Indonesia like tempeh and tofu in Japan, it is endowing these formerly inferior foods with high status.

Yes, this is particularly evident in the case of tofu. We have to keep this in perspective. There are only fifty-five tempeh companies in America, and the total sales of tempeh are relatively small. It's still a very small phenomenon. But tofu is another matter. I know that the popularity of tofu in the United States has had a big influence upon the popularity of tofu in Japan. It may have had a small influence upon the popularity of tempeh in Indonesia; but at least the act of recognition—of Americans saying "Hey!! This is good stuff!" influences people to look at it with new eyes.

So, in a sense your Book of Tofu *has not only promoted tofu in the West, but it has also led the Japanese to rediscover it.*

Definitely. I think that our book has had a positive influence upon the appreciation of tofu in Japan. There's no question about that.

The Japanese have become aware that Westerners are beginning to prize tofu as a delicacy.

Yes. There's a funny thing about the Japanese that I think is peculiarly Japanese—when Americans recognize something that is Japanese, the Japanese just love it. They just lap it up. It'll make the front page of the newspaper.

Thanks to you, Americans are studying tofu, and the Japanese are rediscovering it. So you must be quite a hero in Japan.

Well, we have been on N.H.K. Television, which really has no counterpart in the US. It's what eighty percent of the people in Japan watch. Most houses in Japan have television, and we have been on N.H.K. four or five times. So when we would travel in different parts of Japan, people would stop us and say, "Oh! Did I see you on T.V.?"

Bill Shurtleff   39

Why were the Japanese so late to discover tempeh? They are the masters of miso, and the masters of tofu; yet, it wasn't until the nineteen-eighties that they started using tempeh. Yet it's a soyfood that has been kicking around Malaysia for centuries.

That's a very good question. Recently, we've written a book (which we're publishing ourselves), called *The History of Tempeh*. In it we have done an in-depth study of tempeh in Japan. Part of the reason why it never gained acceptance in Japan is that it was made in such a crude way in Indonesia that up until after the end of World War II, the Japanese studied tempeh as a purely microbiological phenomenon. They were more interested in the type of molds that were used in the fermentation process than they were in its nutritional possibilities as a microbiologist would study anything. The first tempeh was made in Japan in 1983, and in the past three years it has become fairly popular — that would be overstating it. It started to become fairly widely known, and it's available here and there; and there are a couple of companies that are making it. So I think it was just a curiosity until — there again I would say that our *Book of Tempeh* played a role in introducing tempeh to Japan. I would certainly say that.

So, it would seem that in order for the Japanese to become interested in tempeh as a foodstuff, tempeh had first to become Westernized, or Americanized, in order to acquire the cachet and prestige of being discovered in the West before the Japanese could appreciate it.

I think that's probably true.

So prestige and status play a great role in the acceptance of foods.

Well, they certainly do in developing countries. If you want to introduce a food to a developing country, the best way to do it is to introduce it to America first. That's one of the reasons why we have concentrated so much of our effort on the United States.

Well, is Japan a developing country?

No, No, but I think it holds true more of developing countries than it does of Japan. In other words, if you want to introduce tofu to India and you have ten years of your life to spend doing it, you would probably do best to go to the United States, and introduce it to the United States. Then the Indian people will take it and introduce it to India, once they see it succeeding in America. That's really true. I think that is a profound lesson in changing other cultures. If it's okay for America, then it's okay for India. If it's not good enough for America, then the Indians won't be interested.

It's like the way the upper classes used to operate in England and Europe until after the first World War. In Europe, it was the aristocracy who set the fashions in dress as well as diet. They acted as food tasters, if you will, as well as tastemakers for the rest of society. As you pointed out this was also true in Japan, where the highest castes, the military and the priestly caste were responsible for introducing new foods into Japanese society. It was the Buddhist priests and the Samurai who prepared the ground for the acceptance of tofu in Japan during the Nara period and the Kamakura period. In America, you yourself were a kind of priestly courier in the sense that you were a Buddhist monk, and you were bringing a sacred food into America. So it seems to follow that pattern.

I'd rather compare myself to Johnny Appleseed. I'm really a fan of Johnny Appleseed. He was a preacher you know. He was a very interesting character. Everywhere he went, he read from the Bible. When I was a child of seven years, I had a record that told the story of his life set to music.

You really took it to heart.

Oh, I could spout the words still. He was a single man and when he wasn't preaching, he spent a lot of his time traveling, and planting apple seeds. One day he came across a snake, presumably in the forest. Panic-stricken, he trod the snake under foot, killing it. But he was so filled with remorse that he wore no shoe on that foot for a long time, in order to punish the foot for stepping on the snake.

That was his "sackcloth and ashes" for forgetting that all creatures are basically one under the sun. To my way of thinking, that was a beautiful episode; but most people regard him as a nut because of it, and because he wore the pot that he cooked in as a bonnet. Those were the two ways that you could identify Johnny Appleseed—he had no shoe on one foot, and wore a tin pot on his head.

It's interesting because Johnny Appleseed provides another case in point of how a religious figure is often the agent for introducing a new food into a society. Here's Johnny Appleseed, who was a preacher, a priestly courier, literally disseminating apples and apple seeds to colonial American society. Tofu was brought to Japan by Buddhist missionaries

*from China. Likewise, it was really popularized in America by you during
your passage as a Buddhist monk. Earlier in the century an attempt to introduce soyfoods to American society was made by Dr. Harry Miller, an
early proponent of soyfoods in the West, who was also a Seventh-day
Adventist missionary, another priestly courier.*

Oh yes! In fact I'm always surprised that our generation of vegetarians
knows so little about the Seventh-day Adventists. It's really a tragedy!
They have done so much in this country for vegetarianism starting back
in the 1880s, and our generation should really be honoring them; but we
never take the time to do it. I should say "they", because "I" have been
very influenced by them, and I have studied their history at great length;
but I'm always surprised at how little other people know about the
Seventh-day Adventists, and how much they've done! They're really a very
remarkable group of people. They keep to themselves. They don't go out
and seek publicity; and they don't say "Hey! I just wrote an article for
Vegetarian Times!" They have their own magazines; they have their own
stories; they don't trumpet their message. But I think it behooves us to
acknowledge their contribution to the vegetarian movement in this country. If one wanted to write a history of vegetarianism, or a history of important people in this field, one certainly would not want to overlook the
Seventh-day Adventists. The things that they've written are really nice.
The work that they've done in starting these vegetarian food companies is
invaluable. Harry Miller is a good example, as is John Harvey Kellogg.

*Kellogg is probably the most extraordinary of them all. He discovered
peanut butter, and the flaking of cereals; he was an early proponent of
soyfoods.*

You bet he was! We have a whole chapter on Kellogg and his work on
soyfoods in the history of soyfoods that we're writing. This has been our
main project for the past five years.

*During his lifetime he was world-famous; but he is virtually unknown in
America today. Even though his name is borne by the most popular
breakfast cereal in America, Kellogg's Cornflakes, Americans are ignorant of his role in developing it.*

Yes, most people don't know anything about John Harvey Kellogg, or
that he was the private physician to five U.S. Presidents; that he built the
most famous hospital in America (in its time) — Battle Creek Sanitarium
in Battle Creek, Michigan. He was one of the most respected surgeons in

America. He was a vegetarian. He raised fifty-three children. Can you believe that? He wrote something like thirty books. He lectured all over the world. And he was totally devoted to vegetarianism. Everywhere he talked, that would be one of his major themes. He called it "biologic living": It was a vegetarian diet, no alcohol, no smoking, plenty of exercise, and service to God.

Another thing that has been largely forgotten is Henry Ford's role in the development of soyfoods.

Here again, Rynn, this is all in this history book that we are writing. We have probably a twenty-page chapter on the history of Henry Ford's work with soy. I have spoken at length with the man, who is still living, who was the key developer of all those projects.

Was that Atkinson?

No, that was Robert Boyer. Atkinson worked with Boyer, and Atkinson had his own important role to play; but Boyer was the main person who was in charge of it all. He tells many interesting stories about Henry Ford. Anyway, we have a long chapter on Henry Ford. If you had lived back in the thirties, you would certainly have known about Henry Ford and the soybean, because his publicity for soybeans gained national prominence. He was in all the best magazines, frequently talking about soybeans. He built a car with the body made out of soybeans, and he wore a soybean suit.

He set his chemists to work devising new uses for soybeans.

That's right. Particularly devising new industrial uses. That was his main object.

An entire car was fashioned out of soybeans.

That's right. The knobs and so forth, but not the structural parts. Yes. He was very innovative with that.

Also, at the Century of Progress exhibit at the 1934 Chicago World's Fair, Ford served thirty guests a sixteen-course meal in which all the dishes from soup to coffee substitute were made from soybeans.

Yet this is a forgotten chapter of Ford's biography. Americans are simply unaware of it.

That's right.

Benjamin Franklin has been credited with bringing soybeans to America, and with having been the first American to write about tofu. Is this apocryphal?

No, it's true. There's no question about it. The research on that was done by Dr. Ted Hymowitz at the University of Illinois, who is probably the top soybean historian in the world, particularly for the early history of the soybean—a fantastic researcher, a person whom I admire immensely. We tracked the story down, and it's well-documented. But please note: Benjamin Franklin did not introduce the first soybeans to America. He *was* the first American to mention tofu, but he was the second person to introduce soybeans to America. Again, Ted Hymowitz did the research that proved that the first soybeans to come to America were brought by a man named Samuel Bowen in 1765. Samuel Bowen grew soybeans on his estate in Georgia, made soy sauce by the Chinese method in America, exported it to England at high prices, and won a two-hundred guinea prize from the King of England for his fine products. This was before the United States was the United States—before it had won its independence from England.

He was quite a pioneer, wasn't he?

Bowen learned about this because he was a traveler in China. In those days, soy sauce was a real haute cuisine item in Europe. It was a very prestigious seasoning. It was hard to get, and sold for a very high price. So Samuel Bowen reasoned: "Well, I'm one of the few Westerners who's been to China, who knows how to make soy sauce; why don't I grow soybeans in the colonies, make soy sauce, and support myself by exporting it to England where it was highly prized?"

It is a marvelous seasoning. I'm surprised that you and Akiko haven't done a Book of Shoyu *to set beside the others.*

As a matter of fact, we're working on one right now. It's the world's most popular seasoning.

By introducing Americans to tofu, miso, and shoyu, would you say that you've helped to bridge the cultural gulf between Asia and America?

Right, that's one of our expressed objectives: to help bring the best of Asian culture to the United States.

The great poets and thinkers of classical antiquity looked back with nostalgia on a golden age when humans lived at one with the animals and were vegetarians. Indeed, Heian Japan was something of a Golden Age in this sense. Do you think that we will see this Golden Age dawn again?

I often wonder if the vegetarian movement today will parallel the movement to abolish slavery 150 years ago. Within a generation, the abolitionists worldwide changed the idea of buying and selling and keeping slaves from an acceptable one to an abhorrent one. Perhaps we are ready to extend our compassion from slaves to other living creatures as well.

Susan Saint James

Susan Saint James was brought up in the affluent Chicago suburb of Rockford, Illinois, the daughter of a model airplane tycoon. Her father is the founder and board chairman of the Testor Corporation, the internationally renowned manufacturer of model airplanes and model-building paraphernalia. With the exception of Saint James, every other member of the family works for Testor.

As a scion of the founder of Testor Corp., Saint James might have been content to spend her life resting on her inherited laurels. She was a debutante, educated at posh private schools, and until her second year of college seemed destined for the life of a country-club wife. But she was signed by the top modeling agencies of New York and Paris, and used her modeling career as a springboard to stardom in such movies as *Outlaw*

Blues, Love at First Bite, Carbon Copy; in such long-running television series as *The Name of the Game, McMillan and Wife* — and currently *Kate & Allie*. For her television work, Saint James has won an Emmy Award, plus nine Emmy nominations, prompting one wag to remark that her new series should more aptly be called "Kate & Emmy".

Toward the end of the *"McMillan & Wife"* series, Saint James was earning $75,000 per episode. She had the financial acumen to invest some of her earnings in the Celestial Seasonings Tea Company, whose stock has risen dramatically since the company was founded in 1971. Every summer she serves as Mistress of Ceremonies for the Red Zinger Classic bicycle race: held in Boulder, Colorado, it awards the richest purse in American bicycle racing.

When Saint James is not playing the part of a divorced working mother in the top-rated, prime-time TV series *Kate & Allie* — she is playing the role of a happily married mother on a sprawling estate in Litchfield, Connecticut, where she lives with her third husband, TV producer Dick Ebersol; four kids (Sunshine, Harmony, Charlie, and William James); Saint James's parents; and a golden retriever — in a sort of real-life situation comedy that is far too winsome and adorable for prime-time TV.

How long have you been a vegetarian?

I became a vegetarian in 1969.

What kind of vegetarian are you?

I eat eggs and dairy products, but no animals. I never was a big meat-eater anyway. About eight and a half years ago, my husband and I decided to stop eating meat and then about six months later we stopped eating fish. This seems to be the way that most people do it, and it just happened for us naturally that way.

What inspired you to become a vegetarian?

Partly because of my attitude towards health, and partly because of my husband's attitude toward animals. He's such an avid animal lover that, slaughtering them for food, he felt, was a worthless endeavor. I came to it from the point of view of someone who likes to be healthy, energetic, and vital. Together we both came to the same conclusions, but from different viewpoints, and eventually our reasons began to mingle. I began to share his attitude about animals and he began to appreciate the physical rewards of being a vegetarian.

In view of all the medical propaganda about animal protein being essential to human existence, did you have any misgivings about not getting enough protein in your vegetarian diet?

I've never been one to worry, and my husband saw to it that we had protein drinks—soybean protein—every three or four days, and I made a lot of casseroles with nuts and seeds. We eat sunflower seeds with all our breakfast cereals and with our salads at night. It just never was a big debate; it was never a problem with us. A lot of people worried more for us about it than we did ourselves. I had two beautiful births as a vegetarian; they were great labors—no bleeding, no complications, no problems. The diet worked perfectly for me.

What do you usually eat in the course of a day?

For breakfast, either fruit, grains, granola, or cracked wheat cereal, or some kind of eggs. For lunch, I usually have fresh fruit, yogurt, and cottage cheese, or sprouts and cottage cheese with avocados and salad dressing, sunflower seeds, maybe almonds and raisins if it's fruit. For dinner, we usually have a casserole and a salad or a baked potato and a salad; we don't eat a lot of different kinds of foods at one time.

Mostly, we eat fresh foods. We never have any canned foods in the house at all. Every once in a while, though, when I'm in a hurry, I'll make "vegeburgers"—fake hamburgers that come in a box. As a matter of fact, they're on the menu for tonight.

You have no problem, then, obtaining the kinds of foods you like to eat.

We, who live, in California, are spoiled because we have stores like Erewhon here—there's another one in Boston—and it's the best grocery store in the universe. Their store is unique: every single piece of food that's for sale, including all vegetables, has on it the name of the farmer who grew it, so that you could go down to his farm and check on his methods if you were of a mind to do so. They're of such a high quality that you can buy anything in there and be certain of getting products that contain no animal ingredients and no white sugar. They sell a lot of tofu and miso, the Japanese meat substitutes made from soy protein.

What changes did you notice when you switched to a vegetarian diet?

I would say that sticking with my diet through thick and thin—working on location in countries where meat and fish were the only staples, and the temptation to eat fish has been almost irresistible—has been a great source of comfort and strength to me. Just sticking with it has been a stabilizing influence in my life.

Eating fish, I am sure, would not have killed me. I grew up on hot dogs, hamburgers, roast beef, and stuff like that, and I've always been healthy. I have a solid constitution; it certainly wouldn't kill me to have a bite of fish now and then. But just the sheer grit and determination that it takes to stick with this decision in spite of all the temptations—and they can be powerful—have really been a solace to me. It's really a very nice feeling.

I gather your children have been vegetarian since their gestation.

That's right! They're as healthy as horses. They have gorgeous teeth, beautiful skin, beautifully developed slender bodies. And they're very bright. "Lack of protein" certainly hasn't hindered the development of either their looks or their intelligence. I don't want to bore you with superlatives, but their behavior is exemplary. They're full of energy, and they're very alert and sharp-witted. They get their share of protein from vegetable sources, but they don't get an overabundance of protein at all.

When your children began to eat solid foods what did you feed them?

Oh bananas, and cottage cheese, and avocados and yogurt and mashed-up strawberries. I never used commercial baby foods. I have this little gadget called the "baby grinder" and you can take it right into a restaurant, and whatever you're eating you toss into the grinder and it comes out mushy. You just feed them right out of that; it makes one serving.

I understand that you gave birth to one of your children at home.

My daughter was born in the hospital, naturally, and nobody touched me but my own doctor, who was a fascinating eighty-two–year–old woman. But I thought, "Why am I doing this? What am I doing here in this neon green building, with its forbidding atmosphere?" It just isn't the sort of place where you would want to be brought into the world if you had your pick. So I had my son at home and my doctor came to the house to deliver him. Now, most of her work is home-deliveries. I'm so glad that I was born into a time when the knowledge of natural childbirth, and of natural foods, is becoming available.

I notice that you are a member of La Leche League.

Yes, La Leche League is the breast-feeding ladies. They're a very strong organization that I thoroughly support and admire.

Are there many vegetarians among the La Leche ladies?

No, they're just a group of very straightforward ladies who believe that nursing is the single most important factor in a child's development, with which I heartily agree. On the other hand, they admire my position on vegetarianism and they're starting to take more of an interest in what they eat because being so intelligent and well-versed on the subject of infant feeding, they are more open to the whole concept of food and diet reform than the average person might be.

With you and your husband both being vegetarian, has this made your marriage more harmonious?

Well, he's filed for a separation and divorce, so I don't know! No, I don't think it helps. It's a nice common ground, but for the last couple of years I think the only thing that has been holding it together is the fact that I have all the good vegetarian recipes!

For biographical background information about you, I recently came upon a magazine article which mentioned that you were born with the proverbial "silver spoon" in your mouth.

I know, I read it, but that's not really accurate. You know, my father was a toolmaker and worked his way up. I wasn't born into it; I just grew along with my Dad. He was very successful, but nothing compared to the people whom I deal with here in Hollywood, the film industry tycoons. But I did have my debut and things like that when I was in high school. I'm not ashamed of it, because there's nothing wrong with being able to do well in the world and to have material advantages.

What about your relatives—are any of them vegetarian?

Well, my mother eats no meat though she does eat fish. My sister is a total vegetarian. My sister-in-law eats very little meat and my brother almost never eats meat, except for an occasional Fourth of July hot dog. In general, red meat has been eliminated as a staple in the diet of everyone in my family.

Due to your influence?

Partly, and partly because it seems to be that we have developed along the same lines quite by coincidence. We have stumbled upon the same literature and information. They're living, many of them, very far away geographically, yet they have arrived at the same feelings and ideas as I, very much on their own—which is nice. I am sure that we have influenced each other, but I give them full credit.

In your work, have you ever persuaded any cast or crew members to swear off meat? For instance, what did Rock Hudson, your co-star in "McMillan & Wife" think of your diet?

Rock eats the way I ate growing up. Very simple foods which I think benefit him a lot. He thought my diet was something foreign. He understood it but he really wasn't terribly impressed by it because he is a very careful, a very simple eater, himself; but he did eat meat. People have been impressed over the years by my stamina, but, no, I can't think of anyone who suddenly gave up meat because of me.

Of course, through your appearances on talk shows you may have influenced millions of people without knowing it.

Yes, of that I do have some proof because I've gotten torrents of mail from people writing in for vegetarian recipes and the names of vegetarian cookbooks. But I think that they were people who were already a little bit inclined that way first; nothing falls on deaf ears.

Perhaps you planted a seed, though.

That's true. It only takes the first time that people hear about it to set them thinking.

Marty Feldman told me that California was the happiest place in the world for a vegetarian. Do you agree?

Sure. I can walk two blocks from where I live and bump into a great restaurant. The vegetarian restaurants here are sensational. We have a place in Santa Barbara that serves all-vegetarian pizza. They also serve spaghetti and meat balls in which the meat balls are made of fake meat. At another great restaurant they serve turkey sandwiches that contain fake turkey slices—to which I'm addicted. Another is a fancy restaurant with six vegetarian entrees on the menu.

So I guess you and your family can do what it still isn't possible for most vegetarians throughout this country to do—dine out in restaurants that are vegetarian.

Yes. One place serves the most delicious beer. I like beer.

So you're not a teetotaler?

No, there are the same ingredients in beer that you have in bread. And I like the feeling of relaxation it produces.

Are you steadfast in your vegetarianism? What about when you're invited to dinner parties?

Yes. I'm not one of these people who is a vegetarian at home but becomes a meat-eater at social functions. There are people who do that: there are a lot of part-time vegetarians who claim that they eat meat at dinner parties because they don't want to embarrass their hostess or something. But I just won't go unless I've made my position clear. But I tell people in advance. It's not a secret. And if they don't want to have me as a vegetarian, then I'd rather not go anyway.

You see, as a vegetarian, I also feel that dinner parties are an opportunity for me to set an example. The people who sit next to you may never even have heard the word "vegetarian" in their life, and this is their opportunity to inspect one at close range and see that a vegetarian is an otherwise normal human being who simply chooses not to eat meat. It's a chance to set an example for people who eat meat. It opens them to the possibility of vegetarianism—which I think is very exciting.

Do you wear articles of clothing fashioned from animals?

My husband goes so far as not to wear anything made of leather. I did that for a while, but in my business it's just prohibitive. It's too difficult for me to keep it up since they buy clothes and I can't always match them up. But in my offstage, offscreen life, I wear almost no leather except shoes.

It must be difficult to find non-leather shoes.

Well, you see in California it's not too hard, because for the most part I wear sandals and slip-ons. But when I have to wear fashionable footwear in movies or when I'm working in places like New York, then I do find it a little more difficult. My husband has no problem with it at all. He just has all-canvas boots made and as he is not an entertainer, he doesn't have to be a fashion plate. He wears nothing that is made of leather.

Because of the nature of your business you have to wear leather from time to time, but what about fur?

Oh no! I never wear fur of any kind ever! And nobody was allowed to wear fur on "McMillan & Wife"—it was in my contract. I don't even wear suede; I mean to say, I have worn it, but I don't any more. I never owned a fur.

You're probably aware that most cosmetics contain animal ingredients. As an ethical vegetarian how do you cope with that?

There's no way around that for me because I can't control what the make-up men use on me. Although I have tried to use some of the make-ups that are pure, especially lipsticks, because the whale really gets wiped out for lipstick.

Do you attribute any of your success as an actress to your diet?

No; to be fair, I think the only thing I can attribute to my diet is that I was able to nurse two children on the set, and work every single day and learn lines and do all the cooking for my family, because I had such a good diet. With a nonvegetarian diet, I think I would have gone under. I held myself to such a high standard in caring for my children that I insisted on having them with me on the set every day. It was really very trying, very draining, but, because of my diet, I had the strength and the stamina to carry on.

Do you think a vegetarian diet may help to reduce stress?

Oh, definitely. I think that your digestive system has such an easy time of it when you eat vegetarian food and raw food. The bowels function well, and the body isn't overburdened with protein. I've *never* been one of those protein fanatics.

And sugar, I think, is even more lethal than meat. It's one of the biggest killers in the country. It's such a stress encourager.

And so you substitute honey, is that it?

Yes. And honey of course is a body-builder; it's a life–giver.

I understand you're a stockholder in Celestial Seasonings. Did your interest in herbal teas stem from your ideas about health?

In a way. I'm far from being an expert on herbs, but I do know that there was a time when doctors were considered holy men and they healed with herbs. They understood man in his relation to the earth and nature. Now it's just a question of whoever can afford the best university and excel on a test. It's become too mercenary. It's not the same occupation that it was before.

Otherwise doctors would be prescribing a vegetarian diet.

Definitely! Actually my interest in Celestial Seasonings began when I started trying to reduce the stimulants in my life. Coffee was a very, very big hook for me. I still have it occasionally; it's very difficult for me to give up altogether. I drink it with lots of milk and honey, but it's still not a good beverage at all. It masks your emotions. It can really fool you. The worst thing about caffeine is that it masks your fatigue. It's much better to admit the fatigue and go to bed than to keep pushing on.

I read recently that you had officiated at the Celestial Seasonings "Red Zinger Bicycle Race" in Boulder, Colorado.

Oh yes. I was sort of the Mistress of Ceremonies. It was so much fun. It's an incredible sport. Two vegetarians, Dale Stetina and his brother, Wayne, finished first and second in the Race. There was a lot of talk about vegetarianism at the Red Zinger. I think that athletes in the endurance sports like bicycle racing and long distance running, which require lots of stamina, are becoming more interested in it. Also, my husband and I are very sports-minded and we know a lot of other athletes. We've noticed that they have long since gone from having a pre-game dinner of steak to having a pre-game meal of macaroni and cheese. So many athletes find that the carbohydrate meals are much more valuable for endurance than the high protein meals.

You spent several years in your early teens and twenties in Paris as a fashion model.

Yes. It was fabulous; I loved it.

Do you see any relationship between haute couture *and* haute cuisine?

I don't think people are that sophisticated in their thinking. I think it all goes together, but I don't think that it's on purpose. In other words, I think that the people who eat the best meat are often the same people who wear furs, but I don't think it's a conspiracy or anything like that.

These are also usually the same people who like to go hunting. I've noticed this with so many families that have money, that the art and the skill of hunting have been a family tradition for generations. And since hunting is so much a part of their lives, they resent the fact that I or anybody else is a vegetarian, because it detracts from their family traditions and it detracts from the thrill of the sport for them— although where either the thrill or the sport is in hunting, I don't see. Because hunting goes back so far in so many families' histories, it's hard to blame these people for it in 1988. It's equally hard to change their minds about it.

You own a tract of land in the wilds of Oregon on which you've built a vacation retreat and an animal refuge. Is there much hunting in the area?

Not on our property, of course. But they do in Oregon. In the National Forest, they do a lot of hunting as well. Hunting, don't forget, is a very big source of revenue for many of the states.

Through licensing?

The licensing, yes. So you're not only fighting the townspeople's individual feelings, but you're also fighting City Hall. We've never allowed hunters to come anywhere near our property, and although the people who owned the property before us weren't vegetarians, they were devout animal lovers who were opposed to hunting and took care of wounded animals. So when we arrived, there were seventeen deer who would eat right out of your hand.

I also heard that you were helping to protect polar bears.

What happens is that these polar bears stroll through this little town in Alaska; sometimes they're peaceful but sometimes, like humans, the males like to raise a little hell when they hit town, so they're often shot. But the polar bear, as a species, is verging on extinction, and every time one of them is shot, it threatens the survival of the species. So I'm involved with a group that airlifts the bears over the town.

From your experience with violence against animals, do you think that humans are innately violent?

Definitely not. I think diet has a lot to do with it—diet plus breeding and training. People blindly follow the traditions of their culture and their family without stopping to consider that animals are being killed. Also, not breast feeding children, and failing to teach them how to love and show affection, have also helped to create this loveless, alienated society that we live in.

Many of the great poets and thinkers of classical antiquity looked back with nostalgia upon a Golden Age in which warfare and cruelty were unknown, and humans were vegetarian. Do you think that the vegetarianism that is starting to spread throughout the world will usher in a new Golden Age?

I certainly hope so! But I don't know; I don't know if it will really take over. There are just so many meat-eaters and potential meat-eaters in the world. And I've met some really rotten vegetarians! I don't think you can count on their being necessarily more compassionate. That's like saying that all people who meditate are great, or all people who do anything are superior to the ones who don't. A lot of people are vegetarians by design, and yet they haven't worked on their person-alities at all. For the most part, what I think it does is to give you a healthier outlook because you are eating healthy food, and as a result you oftentimes develop a healthy personality. But it doesn't always work that way.

It's not a panacea.

No. I've known a lot of vegetarians who are very hostile towards meat-eaters, and I really despise that; I resent that a lot. If you've found the secret to good health within yourself, that doesn't mean that other people are inferior because they haven't. I have no animosity toward meat-eaters. Some of my best friends are meat-eaters. They just don't have the nutritional awareness that I have, but I don't fault them for that.

From your readings, do you think that meat eating actually causes disease?

I think it's not so much the meat itself but what goes into the meat.

The hormones and chemicals with which the meat is impregnated?

Yes. And I think that meat itself is a massive depressant. It drags you down, physically and mentally, because there is something unwholesome and sinister about the concept of slaughtering animals for food. The blood-letting involved in meat-eating is just outrageous.

Do you think the practice of killing and eating animals affects the personality?

Yes. And I think that it's unnecessary in 1988. The world would be a much better place without it.

Dennis Weaver

D ennis Weaver is a man of many parts who has defied being pigeon-holed in any of the roles that he has played so convincingly. For nine years on the television series *Gunsmoke,* he portrayed the simple-minded, game-legged deputy marshal, Chester, with such authority that audiences were startled to learn that the off-screen Weaver was a strikingly hand-some, former Decathlon champion, and a serious actor. Weaver studied acting in college at the University of Oklahoma and at the Actor's Studio in New York along with Marlon Brando, Paul Newman, Cloris Leachman, Robert DeNiro, and others. For a number of years, he served as director of the Dennis Weaver Actor's Workshop—the only Hollywood actor's school that staged plays for the public.

Born in Joplin, Mississippi during the depths of the Depression, he still remembers the mortification he felt at being the only boy in town who stood in bread-lines to buy day-old bread for his family. It was not until he entered college that he could claim to own more than a single change of clothes and a pair of shoes. He vowed that if he ever became successful, he would do something to help youngsters in his predicament. Shortly after he landed his role in *Gunsmoke,* he set up a "Shoes and Pants" fund for needy students at Missouri Southern State College.

In 1945, after college and two years in the Navy, Weaver married his college sweetheart, Gerry. Weaver and his wife never faltered in their belief that he had the ability to succeed as an actor. They clung together through the odd jobs, the fitful paychecks, the hardships of the early years, and in the early 1950s, he won the role of Chester in *Gunsmoke.*

After nine years in the part, however, Weaver began to chafe and grow restless. Turning his back on the security of the *Gunsmoke* series, he cast about for more challenging roles. Directly after leaving *Gunsmoke* Weaver was offered the leading role in his own series, *Kentucky Jones,* in which he played a veterinarian who adopted a Chinese orphan. He then went on to play a game warden in charge of a 700 pound bear in the *Gentle Ben* series. Then in 1970, he got the chance to play Marshal Sam McCloud in the *McCloud* series, dispelling once and for all the typecasting to which he had been subjected.

Following *McCloud,* for which he won three Emmy nominations and enduring fame, Weaver went on to star in three TV movies—"Ishi—The Last of His Tribe"; "Amber Waves"; and "Duel"—that noted *Washington Post* TV critic Tom Shales rated among the "Top Ten Television Movies Ever Made."

As early as 1958 Weaver stopped eating meat, and thus became the first major actor in the West to embrace a vegetarian diet. Decades before such a way of life would become fashionable, he became a vegetarian, explored Eastern religions, and began to meditate. One Sunday a month, Weaver addresses the Self Realization Temple of the Lake Shrine in Los Angeles, where, as lay minister, he preaches a sermon to overflow audiences.

How long have you been a vegetarian?

Since 1958.

What sort of vegetarian are you?

I'm a lacto-vegetarian.

Have you noticed any changes since you became a vegetarian?

Oh, very definitely; I think it's improved my general health and feeling of well-being, without a doubt.

Have you "converted" anyone else?

I don't do that. I'm not a proselytizer. I don't mount a stump and wave a vegetarian banner. If people look at me and say, "How does he keep so trim?" and "How is it that he's never sick?" and "The flu bug doesn't bite him as it does everybody else!," pretty soon perhaps they'll say, "Well, maybe it has something to do with what he eats!"

Did your wife become vegetarian at the same time you did?

Not at the same time, but eventually she did.

What about your children?

Over the years they have eliminated most flesh foods from their diet. My oldest son, for instance, eats fish, but he doesn't eat beef, veal, or pork, which are the worst, and eventually maybe he'll eliminate fish. My middle son is the same way. However, my youngest son still eats meat. My wife is a very inventive cook and a very tolerant, understanding person. A long time ago we agreed that we would not impose our ideas forcibly onto our children, that we would try to influence them through reason, and through our own example. But we wouldn't try to say this is what you must do, because that always creates an attitude of "heck I won't!" and it usually backfires.

Do you think that major diseases such as heart-disease and cancer may be causally related to meat-eating?

Yes, I do. I don't mean to imply that it's the only factor, but what we eat is certainly a contributing factor to both of these diseases.

Are you concerned about getting enough protein everyday?

I don't measure it out with a scale, but I see to it that I get an adequate amount in the form of cheese, eggs, seeds. You know, vegetables contain a lot of protein, too, which is something that people tend to overlook. Also, we use a vegetarian protein powder. Every so often I'll toss some into the blender with a large glass of orange juice and a few ground almonds—that makes a wonderful drink.

For instance, what do you usually have for lunch?

Oh it varies. It's usually a green salad that may include seeds, ground nuts, assorted fresh vegetables with maybe some cheese sliced into it. Yogurt, cottage cheese, apples, watermelon, whatever's in season.

You were one of the first major film or stage actors to become a vegetarian, were you not?

So far as I know; I was doing it before it was popular.

Do you feel that your diet has enhanced your ability as an actor?

Well, of course, if you enjoy good health, you can be much more creative, because your mind is not distracted by physical ills and disabilities; your mind is free to concentrate.

Why do you suppose the acting profession boasts so many vegetarians?

I think it's for two reasons. I think that perhaps it's more publicized when an actor becomes a vegetarian. Also, on the whole, actors are more prone to experiment. In the first place, they have the kind of questing nature that has led them into this field. They're very eager to open themselves to varied experiences, so when somebody comes along and make a pretty good case for vegetarianism, I think that the actor, or the person with a creative bent, is more apt to give it a chance. By tradition they're supposed to be a little off-beat, so it's easier for them to experiment.

Perhaps another reason is the fact that actors' bodies, and physical appearance are their stock and trade and, like a musical instrument, must be finely tuned to give a good performance. Athletes for the same reason are experimenting with diet.

There's no question about it. I think more and more people are beginning to realize the importance of the fuel that they put into their bodies. Of course, a lot depends on the quality of the vegetarian diet. You could eat nothing but white bread and still claim to be a vegetarian, but you wouldn't be getting the proper nourishment. It's not just a question of eating vegetables and fruits. They must be fresh; they must have retained their vitality. Because if you take vegetables, toss them in a pot, and boil them to death, they're robbed of their nutritional values. And, it's a mistake to think that if you go to the supermarket and fuel up on canned vegetables, that you're going to improve your diet.

You really have a foot in both camps, having been a decathlon star in college. Do you think vegetarianism might have improved your athletic performance?

I wish I knew as much about nutrition then as I do now because I can remember in those days feeling frustrated at not being able to get the maximum performance from my body.

Do you forsee a future generation of vegetarian college athletes setting new records?

What we eat is very important, of course, but along with that there are other things that have to be considered. I think you have to give as much weight to new training methods, techniques, and equipment, and, most of all, to new mental attitudes that come from the realization that it can be done. The mind is really the architect of our body. That's why our mental attitude is almost as important as what we eat in reaping a good harvest on the diet.

You are a lay minister at the Self-Realization Temple of the Lake Shrine. Does the Self-Realization Church advocate vegetarianism among its members?

They suggest it; they say this is the best way to eat for improved health. But they don't require it, and it's not one of the tenets of the church. But you will find that most of the people who are regular members and have sustained their membership for any length of time are vegetarian.

Do you think that meat-eating interferes with self-realization?

Well, I do, of course; that's one of the main reasons why I've eliminated it. However, I was a vegetarian before I joined the Self-Realization Fellowship. I became a vegetarian in the early part of 1958, and I started attending services at the church in the latter part of 1958.

So the late 1950s were a time of great ferment in your life.

There was a five-year period where I made some drastic changes in my lifestyle, starting with my giving up smoking in 1956. At almost the same time, at the suggestion of my dentist, I quit all refined foods. You see, I stopped eating refined foods before I stopped eating meat.

But the change in my eating pattern was gradual. I think it's important for people to understand that there are certain people whom I would classify as habitual vegetarians: those who have a vegetarian heredity or ancestry, who may have fallen away from the diet for a generation, or so, but who are nevertheless more prone to vegetarianism and who can easily do without fish, meat, or poultry. But there are other people for whom it isn't so easy. Generally, people should proceed cautiously when they change their eating habits. It should be an evolving process, so that there is no abrupt cut-off, because the system is accustomed to certain things, and when it is deprived of those things, even if they're bad things, the habit is so ingrained that sometimes there is a negative reaction.

The point I want to make is that we are not all the same, and what is good for one is not necessarily good for another. We're all individuals. You can't make out a menu like a blanket and cast it over everybody; it's just impossible. You should adjust your diet to your specific constitution and your specific needs, keeping in mind that, as far as I'm concerned, vegetarianism is the most correct eating style that we can adopt.

I read somewhere that your family dentist had remarked that a proper diet could put doctors out of business.

He was really referring to the refined foods in our diet: refined sugars, refined rice, and refined wheat. After all of those foods have been depleted of the nutritional value in the refining process, what's left is mostly starch and sugar.

And this attacks the teeth.

Yes, the teeth, the liver, the heart and other vital organs in the body as well. I had been complaining to my dentist that every six months I would invariably have two or three cavities, and this is what prompted him to remark that I should eliminate all the refined foods from my diet.

Have your teeth improved?

That was in 1956. Since then, I've had maybe three small cavities and that would be a generous estimate. It was almost miraculous. But I was very strict; I eliminated candybars, chewing gum, ice cream, pies, cakes, desserts—everything that contained refined sugar.

Do you think that humans are vegetarian by nature?

Yes, but I think our eating habits over many, many centuries have altered that. I say that because we are built like a vegetarian; our physiological equipment is that of a vegetarian; our intestines are long, like those of a vegetarian; our teeth are like a vegetarian's; our appetite is like a vegetarian's. For example, the things that we are naturally attracted to by smell are those things like fruit that grow on a tree; we grow them in our front yard. But the things that we are not naturally attracted to, like meat, we obtain from animals that we slaughter in some remote area of our community where we can't see it, smell it, or hear it. We are repelled by the sight and the smell of blood, whereas a true carnivore is excited by it. These are just some common-sense reasons that led me to feel that I wasn't built to eat meat.

I was interested to read that in your television series Gentle Ben, *the bear refused to eat hot dogs.*

Yes, our bear was a vegetarian. There was a scene in which he was supposed to devour a hot dog, and he wouldn't have any part of it. He wouldn't eat meat. In order to give the illusion that he was eating hot dogs, we had to make them out of a vegetarian product; as soon as we did, he gobbled them right up. I guess it illustrates the power of habit; the foods that you get accustomed to are the foods that you're going to eat and like; the foods you grow up with; the foods that you see your family eating from babyhood. And in this case, the bear got used to bread, milk, berries, fruit, and that's what he would eat.

As you probably know, most anthropologists and archaeologists claim that mankind passed through a hunting stage in prehistory.

Man is a very adaptable creature, and if the food supply was such that the only thing he had to eat was meat, he would adapt to it. I'm sure with a little judicious disguising, he could make it seem very palatable. That's why we still smoke it, barbecue it, roast it, and flavor it with ketchup, sauces, salt, pepper, and other spices. Very few people have gotten accustomed to eating it raw.

Do you think man is innately violent?

No, man is innately a creature of love. That love is the most powerful force in the universe, and eventually—it's a very slow process—it will conquer. I think there will come a time, and this is down the road a great many years, when civilized people will look back in horror on our generation and the ones that have preceded it: the idea that we should eat other living things running around on four legs, that we should raise them just for the purpose of killing them! The people of the future will say "meat-eaters!" in disgust and regard us in the same way that we regard cannibals and cannibalism.

You must feel that way already.

Of course I do! At the same time, I'm not the kind of person who isn't tolerant of other people's lifestyles and eating habits.

Some of your best friends are non-vegetarians.

Oh absolutely! I have a lot of dear friends who are meat-eaters.

You've been very fortunate so far in that none of your major dramatic roles has required that you portray a character that would compromise your ethical principles.

No, but in their original form many of my roles might have, if I had gone ahead and done what was in the script. For instance, in the original movie that was shot as a pilot for *McCloud,* the character was supposed to roll his own cigarettes. The characteristic wasn't so vital to the script or the story that it couldn't be eliminated; so I said, "I won't do this." That's where the match came from that I carried in my hat, and every once in a while I would chew on it. I used to know a lot of people who did that. I said, "If you want that kind of habit, that kind of nervous trait for him, this is it." So it was authentic and it meshed with the character very well.

I've had scripts in which I was supposed to eat meat. Rather than cut it from the script, I would use a meat substitute. Sometimes champagne will be in the script, or scotch-on-the-rocks, or some other alcoholic beverage. As a fictional character I will drink it, but the actual ingredient of course is always a healthy one; the champagne is a non-alcoholic grape juice with a natural carbonation that sparkles and fizzes—made from unfermented champagne grapes. I usually replace liquor with organic apple juice or a similar fruit beverage that has been diluted. I once did a *McCloud* where, in a crucial part of the story, I had to drink beer. Now beer is very difficult to fake because of the head, the foam; but they have a product in Australia—we don't have it here—that resembles beer and is made from herbs, called "Australian Beer." It tasted rather funny, but it wasn't bad after you got used to it, and it did look exactly like beer.

What would you do if you were asked to portray a big-game hunter or to participate in a hunting scene?

It would depend entirely on the script: what kind of story it was; how it was utilized; what the net result of the story would be; whether or not it would be an affirmative position, a constructive position. You see, I separate myself, Dennis Weaver, from the actor. I cannot limit myself on screen to what I do in real life; that's sheer foolishness. Then I'm no longer an actor, I am simply portraying myself on screen which would be very dull. So if the character I play is the kind of person who could shoot a buffalo, and it's required in the story to make a particular point, I would have no qualms about doing that.

Is there an alternative for an actor who doesn't wish to wear leather or leather shoes?

None that's acceptable right now.

Let's imagine that you're on location in Texas, and a fan, having watched you in Gunsmoke *and* McCloud, *invites you to his ranch for a big barbecue.*

I'm laughing because it happens all the time. When I was on *Gunsmoke,* particularly, I used to go on a lot of personal appearances, playing rodeos and state fairs and inevitably the sponsor would try to make my stay as pleasant as he could by arranging for a big barbecue and blow-out. What I found worked for me is that whenever I'd get off the plane, or during my first contact with the public relations people or the sponsor who is connected with the project, I would always say, "Look, I'm one of those strange Hollywood people; you've got to put up with me—I don't eat meat." When I put it in terms that conveyed, "I'm the strange one and you're the sane one, but you've got to condone my idiosyncracies because I'm an actor and I'm wierd," there was no problem after that. They would rustle up all sorts of salad mixes, and fresh fruit and cheese. They were very understanding. Also, as the character of Chester on *Gunsmoke*, I was an habitual coffee-drinker; that was one of the traits that made him so identifiable; he was always making this special coffee which was vile, and no one would drink it but Chester. So when I would go on personal appearance tours, people would offer me coffee, and I'd say, "I never drink it," and that would really boggle their minds.

The point is, I've never tried to hide my vegetarianism; I've usually tried to make a joke out of it.

If this country becomes increasingly vegetarian, do you think that we will lose our fascination with the cowboy, whose function was to herd cattle?

No, I don't think that will happen at all. I think that as time goes by, fascination for that period in our history will even grow. It will have nothing to do with whether we become vegetarian or not. My interest in it has not decreased since I've become a vegetarian.

Do you think the vegetarianism that is gaining ground in America will be at the expense of the cattle interests?

I think it's just a naturally evolving set of circumstances. Probably one of the reasons why vegetarianism is going to be increasingly more and more at the expense of the cattle industry is simply because of the growth of population; the world-wide population boom is an enormous problem. And you can feed far more people on the same piece of ground by making it vegetable-producing rather than by keeping it cattle-producing. So out of necessity, the world is going to resort to vegetarianism just to feed itself.

It would seem that the real peace officers who are taming the West are the spiritual men from the East, like Swami Vivikananda, and Krishnamurti.

I think they are bringing to the West an ingredient that's been missing from our culture; just as we in the West are bringing to India, for instance, an element that has been missing from their culture and for which they've been searching—the initiative we have and the willingness to participate in society. I think both civilizations—East and West—have been out of balance in the past, and now there's a process of equilibrium and exchange between the two which I think is very good. Kipling was wrong; I think "the twain" are meeting because of people like Swami Vivikananda, Yogananda, Schweitzer, Gandhi, and so many others. There's much to be learned on both sides.

In addition to their vegetarianism and their concept of *ahimsa* (non-violence), one of the other features of the Indian heritage that we might do well to adopt is their ability to control themselves, their calmness, and self-possession under pressure. That doesn't mean that we should cultivate indifference to what goes on around us, but we shouldn't feel defeated if we can't always achieve something that we feel is important.

Do you think that the vegetarian diet itself will bring about such a change in attitude?

Vegetarianism in itself helps to promote calmness because it eliminates certain toxins, certain carbons that agitate human beings and make them restless and excitable. But vegetarianism alone will never abolish violence, greed, and all the other evils in the world—not by itself. However, it does provide a help. And I think that things go together in this world, and the person who, for whatever reason, turns to vegetarianism will be all the better physically and mentally for having done so. It might be because they just don't like the idea of killing animals, and if they don't like the idea of killing animals, they're certainly not going to like the idea of killing other human beings.

Do you think that meat is a status food?

In certain societies it is, yes. In our house it's not a status food at all. But among cattlemen it's a great status symbol not only to eat meat, but to be able to throw it away. A cattleman will often butcher a steer, eat the choice cuts, and throw the rest to the dogs or whatever. Also, people will go into a big supper club or into one of the better restaurants and order the most expensive, prime piece of meat. It's like buying a Cadillac, or a pair of diamond-studded cufflinks.

And if you order a big salad, or some sautéed vegetables, they look askance.

Sometimes there's a question as to whether they'll serve you or not because they wonder if they'll be given the proper tip.

The activity of eating seems to be polarized sexually; people are inclined to regard steak as a masculine diet, whereas vegetarianism has been viewed as being either effete or eccentric.

Well, of course, because of all the publicity connected with meat-eating. You know the commercial on television where a fellow meets his friends in a restaurant after a football game. A waiter comes up to take their order and they answer, "No question about it, give me steak and beer!" Well, I mean this is the sort of propaganda that is pumped into us all the time. They would never show someone saying, "I think I'll have sunflower seeds and yogurt."

Do you think the vegetarianism that is starting to spread throughout the world today will usher in a new Golden Age?

Well, I think it's an indication. I don't think that vegetarianism per se is going to do that, but I think that the upward evolution of humanity is suggested by the fact that more and more people are changing over to vegetarianism.

Isaac Bashevis Singer

Twice a winner of the National Book Award, Isaac Bashevis Singer was awarded the Nobel Prize for Literature in 1978.

Singer's enormous popularity and stature in the United States is the more astonishing since his first language—the language in which he thinks and creates—is Yiddish. He once joked that his writing must be 150 percent better than it appears "because you lose 50 percent in translation." Even though Singer speaks German and Polish and has a good command of English, he prefers to write in Yiddish because he feels that "it has vitamins that other languages haven't got." Consequently, he is the first writer to have received a Nobel Prize who writes in a language for which there is no country.

Singer was born July 14, 1904, in Radzymin, Poland. Both of his grandfathers were rabbis as was his father. It is difficult to imagine more unfavorable auspices for a young novelist than to be forced into exile from his native land at the age of 31 with a gift of eloquence in a language that was becoming extinct. Had anyone suggested in 1935 (the year of Singer's emigration to America) that a Polish refugee, writing in a language silenced by the Holocaust, would receive the Nobel Prize for Literature in 1978, Isaac Singer would have been the first to laugh.

Indeed, for several years after he arrived in New York, he was paralyzed with culture shock and unable to write. But when .Saul Bellow translated *Gimpel the Fool* for the *Partisan Review* in 1953, the response was immediate; Singer's stories began to appear in such journals as *Commentary, Esquire, Playboy,* and *The New Yorker.* The Polish refugee who wrote in an endangered language was on his way to winning the Nobel Prize for Literature.

How long have you been a vegetarian?

I've been a vegetarian for fourteen years.

What do you usually eat in the course of a day?

I eat what I like. In the morning I have some skim milk and hard-boiled eggs. For lunch I take a sandwich that consists of toast, sliced tomatoes, and cottage cheese. In the evenings, some vegetables. This is more or less how it goes every day.

Have you felt better since you became a vegetarian?

Since I didn't do it to feel better, I never measure it by that. I feel that I'm right. This is the main thing.

I once read that it was Spinoza's notion that man can do as he likes to animals which repelled you from eating meat.

Yes. I don't say that this passage made me a vegetarian, but I felt, when I read it, a great protest. I thought, if we can do to animals whatever we please, why can't another man come with a theory that we can do to human beings what we please? This did not make me a vegetarian. I was in my mind a vegetarian before—because when I read this I was revolted. And though I love Spinoza and always admired him (and I still do), I did not like this text.

Many of your own stories treat the subject of vegetarianism. Do you use vegetarian leitmotifs intentionally?

I would say that of course I never sit down to write a story with this intention, with a vegetarian tendency or morality. I wouldn't preach. I don't believe in messages. But sometimes if you believe in something, it will come out. Whenever I mention animals, I feel there is a great, great injustice in the fact they are treated the way they are.

I've noticed that you use butchers and slaughtermen to represent evil.

Well, I'm inclined to do so. If a character's a ruffian, I would make him a butcher—although some of them are very nice people.

In the story "Blood," was it your intention to show that people who traffic in animal flesh have something rapacious about them?

What I wanted to show was that the desire for blood has an affinity with lust.

In "Blood," the female character, Risha, first seduces the ritual slaughterer Reuben, then insists on killing the animals herself. She sets up as a nonkosher butcher, and, as though following a logical progression, finally becomes a . . .

She becomes a werewolf.

Do humans who eat meat become predators?

In shedding blood there is always an element of lust.

At the beginning of the story, you mentioned that the Cabalists knew that blood and lust are related, and that's why the commandment "Thou shalt not commit adultery" immediately follows the injunction against killing.

Yes, but I feel so myself. There is always an element of sadism in lust and vice versa.

Do you feel that people who eat meat are just as reprehensible as the slaughterer?

The people who eat meat are not conscious of the actual slaughter. Those who do the hunting, the hunters, are, I would say, in the grip of a sexual passion. Those who eat meat share in the guilt, but since they're not conscious of the actual slaughter, they believe it is a natural thing. I would not want to accuse them of inadvertent slaughter. But they are not brought up to believe in compassion.

I would say that it would be better for humanity to stop eating meat and stop torturing these animals. I always say that if we don't stop treating these animals the way we do, we will never have any rest.

I think other people are bothered by meat-eating too, but they say to themselves: "What can I do?" They're afraid that if they stop eating meat they will die from hunger. I've been a vegetarian for so many years—thank God I'm still alive!

I've also noticed that in "The Slaughterer," you say that the phylacteries . . .

. . . are made of leather, yes. I'm always conscious of it. Even the Torah is made from hide. And I feel that this somehow is wrong.

Then you say, or have the character in "The Slaughterer" say, "Father in heaven, Thou art a slaughterer!"

Didn't we just have an earthquake in Turkey where thousands of innocent people died? We don't know His mysteries and motivations. But I sometimes feel like praying to a vegetarian god.

In your novel Satan in Goray *the woman in the story, Rechele, eventually becomes impregnated by Satan . . .*

Well, she thinks so.

My impression was that she had been prepared for her match with Satan by being raised as the adopted daughter of a slaughterer.

Yes, she was the daughter of a slaughterer.

Was that your intention?

I don't know what my intention was. But now that we talk about it, I realize that I made her father a slaughterer.

And her second husband, he was also a slaughterer.

Her father was a slaughterer, and the one who marries her too. I must have had some reason for it. You'd be surprised, writers don't know really what they are doing.

And this was before you converted to vegetarianism!

Twenty years before.

So you must have had some vegetarian presentiments.

Yes, I always thought about eating meat. These things bothered me all the time.

In Satan in Goray *the town sinks into corruption, the earth fails to yield its crops, and the trees put forth no fruit. But strangely enough, there is a surplus of meat.*

I will tell you: When there is a famine, when the animals have nothing to eat, the people who keep them will slaughter the animals so as to get some profit out of them. Whenever there is a famine, even today, in Russia, when there's not enough food, the peasants slaughter many animals.

So meat is really a famine food, eaten only as the last resort.

When there's a famine of grain and vegetables, there's often an abundance of meat. Of course, this is only for one year. If the famine lasts a few years, the meat will also be gone. But the first thing that the people do when they have nothing to eat, is to slaughter the animals, because they will die anyhow.

It seems to me that a breakdown of the marriages in Goray accompanies the increased consumption of meat.

Well, I wouldn't say that the eating of meat is the cause, but of course in *Satan in Goray,* I make believe that all of these things go together: the slaughter, the adultery, all these things.

But even in The Family Moskat, *which is a domestic saga, animal-slaughter and failed marriages seem somehow interwoven with the health of the community.*

I will tell you: I did not think much about vegetarianism when I wrote

The Family Moskat or *Satan in Goray*. But these things came out through my pen almost automatically.

Do you feel that people who eat meat are evil?

Well, I wouldn't go so far. I don't want to say this about all the people who eat meat. There were many saints who ate meat, very many wonderful people. I don't want to say evil things about people who eat meat. I only like to say that I'm against it. My vegetarianism is in fact a kind of protest against the laws of nature, because actually the animals would suffer whether we ate them or not. Whatever the casé, I am for vegetarianism.

In previous interviews you have stated that like the Cabalists you feel that this is a fallen world, the worst of possible worlds.

This is what the Cabalists believe. I don't know all the worlds. All I can see is that this world is a terrible world.

Do you think meat-eating contributes to the triumph of evil throughout the world?

To me, it is an evil thing—slaughter is an evil thing.

Do you think the world might be improved if we stopped the slaughter?

I think so. At least we should try. I think, as a rule, a vegetarian is not a murderer, he is not a criminal. I believe that a man who becomes a vegetarian because he has compassion with animals is not going to kill people or be cruel to people. When one becomes a vegetarian it purifies the soul.

In an interview that you gave to Commentary *in the mid-1960s, you mentioned that you were something of a scholar in spiritual matters.*

Scholar? I wouldn't consider myself a scholar.

Well, do you think that animal souls also participate in the spiritual world?

Well, I have no doubt about it. As a matter of fact, I have a great love for animals that don't eat any meat.

Many of the great poets and philosophers of classical antiquity look back with nostalgia on a Golden Age in which war, murder, and crime were unknown, food was abundant, and everyone was vegetarian. Do you think that if people became vegetarian again they would become better people?

Yes. According to the Bible, it seems that God did not want people to eat meat. And, in many cases where people became very devout, or very pious, they stopped eating meat and drinking wine. Many vegetarians are anti-alcoholic, although I am not.

I think one loses desire for intoxicants when one becomes a vegetarian; it purifies the body.

I think it purifies the soul.

Do you believe in the transmigration of souls?

There's no scientific evidence of it, but I personally am inclined to believe in it. According to the Cabalists, when people sin, they become animals in the next life, sometimes ferocious animals, like tigers and snakes. I wouldn't be surprised if it were true.

Do you believe in the actual manifestation of demons in the physical world?

I believe it—yes. I mean, I don't know what they are. I'm sure that if they exist, they are part of nature; but I feel that there are beings that we haven't yet discovered. Just as we discovered only about two hundred years ago the existence of microbes and bacteria, there is no reason why we shouldn't one day discover some other beings. We do not know everything that goes on around us.

So you think there are malevolent spirits acting in the world today?

I think there may be such spirits, or astral bodies—I don't know what to call them. Since I've never seen them or contacted them, everything I say is just guesswork. But I feel there may be entities of which we have no inkling. Just the same, they exist and influence our life just as bacteria and microbes did without our knowing it.

Do you think, on the other hand, that there are benevolent spirits?

Yes, I do. There is a great possibility of it.

Do you wear leather and articles of clothing made from animals?

I try not to, but I can never get the kind of shoes that are not though, I'm going to do something about it. What about you? Do you wear leather shoes?

No, I don't wear anything that could cost an animal his life.

Tell me the name of the place where I can get these shoes that you wear.

I can send you the name of a mail order shoe company where you can get them.

Do me a favor and please do.

I shall. There's a mail-order firm in Patterson, New Jersey—The Haband Co.—which makes shoes of nothing but synthetic leather.

They're not to be gotten in stores?

You can get them, if you're willing to make a canvass of all the stores—which can be quite time-consuming—and insist upon buying shoes fashioned entirely from man-made materials.

I never wore furs, and I don't want to wear anything made from animals.

I just think that if one is a vegetarian, one should be consistent.

You are absolutely right, one hundred percent.

Brigid Brophy

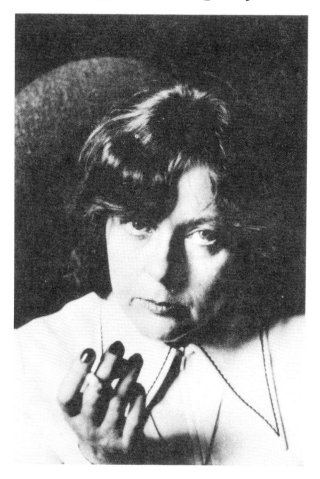

B rigid Brophy was born on June 12, 1929, to a family noted for its intellect. Her father was the noted English author John Brophy, her mother a headmistress and Latin scholar. Her maternal grandfather was an autodidact Greek scholar whose passion for the language was so pronounced that he christened all his children with Greek names of his own devising. From him Brophy inherited her love for Greek literature, in which, along with Latin, she distinguished herself as a Classical scholar at Oxford.

Brophy's literary output has been as diverse as it is rich. She has written short stories, novels, a play, and major critical studies of Mozart, Aubrey Beardsley, and Roland Firbank; she has also examined the destructive and self-destructive impulse in western culture in *Black Ship to Hell* (1962). With her husband, Michael Levey (an art historian and keeper of the National Gallery), and Charles Osborne, she recently collaborated on a witty, iconoclastic reappraisal entitled *Fifty Works of English Literature We Could Do Without.*

Third-generation Irish-English, Brophy is in the best tradition of the brilliant expatriate Irish writers, whose ranks include Jonathan Swift, Oliver Goldsmith, Richard Brinsley Sheridan, Thomas Moore, Oscar Wilde, and Bernard Shaw. With Shaw she shares not only Irish ancestry but also ardent antivivisectionist sympathies. Other traits which the two have in common are a sparkling wit, a fierce outspokenness, and a daunting critical and creative intelligence; moreover, both converted to vegetarianism at the age of twenty-five.

Brophy, however, is the first thinker to have applied the principles of psychoanalysis to humanity's relationship to animals, and to have attempted an analysis of human carnivorism in Freudian terms. This she has done in portions of her book *Black Ship to Hell,* and in an essay which she contributed to a recently published anthology of writings advocating the liberation of animals, *Animals, Men and Morals.*

What prompted you to give up eating flesh?

I think I had always been prompted to, but I didn't have sufficient moral courage to think that I was right until I reached the age of discretion, which was when I was twenty-five.

Did you become a vegetarian immediately? Did you give up fish, flesh, and fowl all at once?

Yes, I became one immediately, as soon as I came to the decision. It coincided, curiously enough, with my getting married. Perhaps I decided that if one was taking important decisions, they would best be taken in the same year. My husband became a vegetarian very much more recently. For a long time, he was a carnivore and I was a vegetarian.

That must have been rather difficult.

Well, it didn't lead to any great ideological scenes, but it did lead to certain practical difficulties.

Did you have to prepare separate meals?

Well, one of us had to prepare two separate meals, yes—he as often as I.

There's no division of labor in the kitchen?

There is no one positively panting to do it; what is done is the minimum that any two people can get away with.

What about your daughter? Did she become a vegetarian?

Well, this was an interesting thing. I was extremely scrupulous; I suffered probably from overscrupulousness and, therefore, I was very careful to put no emotional pressure on my husband, and not to wield the power of being a mother over my daughter. And what in fact happened was that she, in adolescence, went away to stay with some people who, quite unknown to her, were vegetarians. They argued the point and she came to the conclusion that they were right. So back she came, a vegetarian. Whereupon she, who had no emotional scruples, set about my husband terribly hard and converted him instantly, largely by emotional blackmail—which I had abstained from applying all those years.

Do you think that man is innately vegetarian?

You mean, do I think that the first members of the human species were vegetarian? No, I think they were probably omnivorous actually, as most primates tend to be omnivorous; and indeed this may be part of our important flexibility that we've needed.

Morally and ethically, however, this is where the problem arises because we do have a choice. We are capable of subsisting on flesh even though it may be morally repugnant.

Yes.

If it were immediately apprehensible that flesh was poisonous, then . . .

Then that would be a whole lot better for chickens and fish and cows and lambs. But it wouldn't, of course, be morally better for us because we'd have no choice. I don't think one thinks of a deer as being morally superior to the tiger, because neither of them has any choice. But we do have this choice.

How do you feel about the wearing of animal skins, leather shoes, for example?

This can be avoided and should be avoided. I go through shoe shops, picking up shoes and smelling them to see if they smell of leather so that I can avoid them if they do. Do you?

No. The shoes I'm wearing are made of synthetic, man-made materials.

I mean, one is lucky that one lives in an age when there's a quite simple practical solution; it probably wasn't as easy about 1900.

Well, it isn't really easy even now, because they're not very well stitched and they fall apart rather quickly.

On the other hand, they are mainly cheaper, so that one is probably paying the same amount in the end, though having to do it more often.

Non-vegetarians argue that the diet is soporific; it tranquilizes people.

Do they believe that Bernard Shaw was asleep and tranquilized, or indeed Shelley, one of the least tranquil people who's ever existed? No. It's nonsense.

I do think that one's fellow animals of other species are aware of the change in one's own attitude when one becomes vegetarian, even if they themselves are not vegetarian. I don't think they scent about one that doesn't eat meat, but I do think that the psychological act of deciding to be a vegetarian frees one from a lot of guilt towards animals and I think they are aware of this. My impression is that one's relationship to them becomes very much less ambiguous and ambivalent and one is freer to think of them as equals; I think it's this property that they respond to. I definitely have the impression that I have a different relationship with animals since I became a vegetarian, although I was always very fond of them and had a lot around. But I think that they are very aware that one is less ambivalent toward them, and less condescending toward them.

Perhaps they sense that one does not regard them as potential meals.

Yes—and that one is not jealous of them, and that one is not eager to show one's superiority to them. I mean, so many people keep a dog because they want to be able to say "Sit!" and the dog will then sit, thereby demonstrating that they are superior. I think if one has thought out one's relationship to them a bit more thoroughly than that, then one becomes aware that one is not superior to them—only different.

Of course it is partly envy of their freedom, I mean, nobody's going to blame the animals if they go and dig up the neighbor's garden, whereas if you go and dig up the neighbor's garden, the neighbors will certainly have words to say to you. One holds them, I think, very free of moral responsibility.

They don't appear to work, and they seem to lead a life of enviable leisure.

Domestic animals don't work, and wild animals don't appear to.

And of course they seem to have a lot of sexual freedom—which we might envy.

Yes, and which one can't blame them for. I think this is the thing: whatever as a human being you do sexually, someone will blame you for it—whatever you do, or indeed, whatever you don't do.

And of course they are quite beautiful. I wonder if that's why we take their fur, out of envy.

Yes, it must be.

The Jewish-Christian mystic, Simone Weil, once wrote: "The great trouble in human life is that eating and looking are two different operations . . . it may be that vice, depravity, and crime are nearly always, or perhaps always, attempts to eat what we should only look at." Do you think that in eating the flesh of animals we are confusing the operations of eating and looking?

Yes, this is absolutely correct. It's this awful mistake that we make about identification isn't it? I like you, therefore, I'd like to be you, therefore, I'm going to eat you. This childish failure to realize that if you eat the thing you admire, it won't be there any more.

To paraphrase Wilde's comment, "Each man eats the thing he loves."

This is absolutely correct, but to some extent we are gradually learning. We are learning to go on safari with a camera instead of a gun.

To look, rather than to devour.

Yes, and luckily, thanks to the invention of film, there is a possession that you can have at the end. It takes an awful long time to realize that one can appreciate things just by looking. I mean it takes an awful long time to understand that one can appreciate one's friends, or people that one loves in a closer way than that, without wanting to change them. Some people never learn this, and this makes for very fraught relationships. The ultimate way of changing people is to absorb them and make them part of your digestive process.

Freud held that the totem animal sacrificed and eaten at the ancient festivals symbolizes the father, whom all men, as the cultural heirs of Oedipus, wish to devour. In reading your book, Black Ship, *the image comes to mind of patriarchal societies begetting an endless succession of people who are devouring their fathers in the nearest animal surrogate.*

Yes, this is true. It is a book that interprets the aggressiveness of human beings in terms of human beings' antagonism towards the father-figure.

If the eating of animals is a symptom of the Oedipus complex, do you suppose the killing of animals begat the Oedipus complex, or the other way around?

I think the other way around, because the Oedipus complex is at its most violent when one is about three and three-year–olds are unlikely to be very proficient at husbandry and slaughtering. So to that extent, I suppose, probably we were originally carnivorous. If one thinks of a prehuman species which lived on fruit or something of that kind, I don't think that one would say that they were likely to be free of ambivalent feelings toward their fathers. Indeed, I think that one detects these feelings in most mammals: the ghost of an Oedipus situation arises in most mammals, and some mammals are vegetarian.

I wonder if the vegetarian diet can disarm the Oedipus complex.

Yes, because reason can always disarm the irrational. If reason finds itself to be irrational, it can disarm it; and if one finds reason and discovers that eating animals is immoral, unnecessary, and done largely for superstitious reasons, then one is delivered from the compulsion to do it.

Many people are vegetarian *not* for rational motives, as I've described, and I'm certainly not saying that vegetarianism is only good when done rationally, because there are the animals to consider. Any animal that lives its life out as the result of somebody's not eating it, is an advance—no matter how superstitious, irrational, or just plain crazy the person's reason is for not doing it. Therefore, I constantly welcome the increase in what I could call irrational vegetarians. But if one is looking for actual deliverance from various irrational compulsions in the human psyche, than I think one must turn one's head to reason as the only permanent deliverer. A delusional system can deliver you for a certain amount of time, but it's a bit like curing a bodily illness by hypnosis; it will come back in another form later.

The myth that Freud reconstitutes is that of the primal father who exerts a tyrannical sway over the males in the primal horde until they eventually overthrow him. Do we ritually enact primal parricide whenever we sit down to a meal of meat?

Yes. Although it's divested of its ritual significance, the superstition remains absolutely the same: the superstition that, by eating pieces of steak, you acquire the strength and health of the bull is what keeps people being carnivorous. This original superstitious-psychological constellation acquired something extra when people began to believe in evolution because this, in a sense, reinforced the primitive belief that animals are our ancestors which, indeed in a direct scientific sense, they are—at least collaterally. It's a superstition that even quite responsible medical scientists constantly put forward. And it *is* purely a superstition, obviously, with the existence of so many healthy vegetarian humans.

You point out in Black Ship *that the Christian sacramental mass is a revival of the totem feast with Christ serving as a human surrogate for the sacramental lamb.*

Yes, he was the lamb of God.

In Greek religion, a progenitor of Christ would have been Dionysos, who was embodied, hostlike, in the small animals whom the Greek women would tear apart with their bare hands and devour raw during religious orgies.

Yes, and of course Osiris.

I wonder, however, if the Christian sacrament isn't a humane advance on Maenadism and other forms of ancient religious sacrifice.

It is, actually. It's a great ethical advance on both the ancient Jewish sacrifice and the ancient Graeco-Roman sacrifice in that we don't actually sacrifice an animal, but a wafer. What a pity that the Christians didn't go the whole Gadarene hog and stop eating animals as well as stop sacrificing them!

I wonder if, as the cultural heirs of Oedipus, we are bound to slaughter animals indefinitely.

I don't think one can say that such acts are inevitable, because we are capable of changing as a species. If one person can become a vegetarian, there is no reason why the entire human species shouldn't become vegetarian. If Mozart can write those operas, it does not follow that the whole human species can write operas like that, but a norm like vegetarianism is perfectly capable of becoming an acquired characteristic of the whole species.

Slavery was universal; it is now virtually abolished. There are areas where it still happens, but the entire consensus of world opinion has turned against it; and in those areas where it does exist, it will gradually disappear as they become more educated. Yet three thousand years ago, you wouldn't have found a person who would support this point of view. It would have seemed to them impossibly idealistic.

Classical Greece was predominantly vegetarian. Even the aristocrats, who consumed the most meat, usually only did so at festivals.

Yes, but I think that this is true of Greece even now. If you go to an expensive restaurant, they will be eating meat to show that they indeed have enough money to pay for meat. Then you can go to a very cheap restaurant in a village and the chances are you'll get vegetarian food, because that is what the locals eat. It's cheap.

You think it's primarily economic, then.

Yes, I do, I'm afraid. I wish it were ethical. There *is* a strain in Classical Greek which was vegetarian for reasons of reincarnation, which is what? A mythological approach to an ethical reason. So this obviously did exist in Greece.

Pythagoras, Empedocles, the Orphics, Apollonius, Plutarch, Porphyry, these poets and philosophers wrote poetry and philosophical treatises urging vegetarianism. And yet if one compares this pantheon of Greek thinkers with the sages and the intelligentsia of Europe for almost two thousand years, the vegetarian tradition just doesn't exist, except on the outermost fringe.

In modern history, there have been two waves of it: one at the turn of the century and the other more recent and, interestingly, very much among moral philosophers in the universities. So curiously enough, it looks as if philosophers are at last moving toward philosophy!

Da Vinci was the first modern Western vegetarian that I can think of and then, later, there was Shelley. In his poetry, particularly Queen Mab, *there's a great deal of vegetarian imagery.*

Yes, there were various people before that. There was a man called Tryon in the early part of the eighteenth century; he published a mixed philosophy and cookery book about this. And Pope, though I don't think he was a vegetarian, maybe he was a surreptitious vegetarian, definitely maintains that primitive man was (a) innocent and (b) vegetarian.

You point out in Black Ship *that Pope was an intellectual vegetarian; rather, he accepted it as an intellectual ideal but couldn't put it into effect.*

All those people were in the curious situation of upper-class victims. In the days when the upper class had servants, they were entirely the victims of their servants. It may well be that he simply didn't know how to say to his cook that he wanted from now on to be a vegetarian. People have always traditionally been very compliant with their cooks. The cook was very much needed in the household and, of course, one dare not offend one—especially if it was a good cook—for fear that he or she would up and leave.

Do you think that meat is still a status symbol today?

Yes, undoubtedly.

In America, the steakhouse is a male shrine. I wonder if fruits and vegetables are not conventionally thought to be a diet proper to women, while flesh is held to be a diet proper to warriors and males generally?

Brigid Brophy 87

That is true. The steakhouse is male, and the chophouse is male. That is quite true. But I think this merely dates from the era when women were not supposed to go out to restaurants. Indeed, if you took a woman to dinner, you had to book a secluded room in a restaurant so that, in this oriental way, she should not be seen by the eating public.

Also I think that men who eat vegetarian food have been thought somewhat effeminate in the past.

That I think is true, yes. So what I'm saying is that I've not heard the converse, but—whatever the opposite of converse is—the obverse. Yes, that one has heard. Indeed, wasn't it Mrs. Patrick Campbell who said to Shaw, "If you ever eat steak, God help all women!"

Animal flesh, white flour, and white sugar were highly prized by the European aristocracy in the Middle Ages. Is there a tendency for the foodstuffs prized by the aristocracy or the rich to work their way down the social scale as they become more inexpensive?

Yes, but there is more to meat-eating than that because, when a word, for example, works its way down, or a proper Christian name, the upper class gives it up. For example, the name Mabel, which was an aristocratic name when Oscar Wilde was writing, had become a name for maidservants by the time I was a child. But with meat, because of the superstitions involved, it has worked its way down but the upper class has not given it up.

However, there is a tendency among certain groups to give up meat. I belong to the National Secular Society, which is a free-thinking organization. Whenever they have their annual dinner, or whatever, there's always a space on the booking form for you to fill in if you're a vegetarian. This is probably for historical reasons; it dates from the 1880s and 1890s when progressive people tended to be vegetarian.

Minority groups may tend automatically to partly overlap with vegetarianism and, therefore, they are liable to make provision for vegetarians on social occasions. This is a very good thing: if all minority groups became vegetarian, then vegetarians would become a majority.

But if the middle and lower classes tend to take their cues in speech, dress, manners, and feeding habits from the upper classes, then doesn't this suggest that the upper class will have to become vegetarian?

It would have done up till about 1900. I'm not sure that the whole social thing hasn't altered now. I don't think that the official upper class any longer has a great deal of influence. I think it would be the glamour class: if all the news-readers on television were known to be vegetarian, this might influence people.

There's probably a greater chance now for vegetarianism as a result of this transfer of charisma and prestige from the aristocracy to celebrities if they could be persuaded that vegetarianism was a sound diet.

No, because aristocrats are a good deal freer than other people: they are able to be insolent, eccentric. If they were to be vegetarians, they wouldn't have to apologize at a dinner or warn the hosts in advance. They would simply rise and say, "My God! I can't eat this revolting stuff!" So I think it is easier for them, whereas with a news-reader, it's a two-way reaction, sort of like that of a politician who is terribly frightened of losing votes. So one is left with a class leading society that is terribly afraid of actually leading.

Is there any relation between haute couture *and* haute cuisine?

Yes, and they're both related to the basic peasant economicalness in the French character because French cooking, in fact, consists of making the most economical use of the material that you can make. And likewise I suspect with clothes: how to get the maximum dress out of the smallest bolt of original material. Yes, there is a connection.

But why do rich Americans and rich English women make the pilgrimage to Paris to purchase the latest creation in food or fashion?

Oh, the success of French propaganda. French is the language which invented the word chauvinist; and there is simply an absolutely relentless propaganda about French cooking, clothes, and literature. French literature is so esteemed in this country, which actually has a literature that is five-hundred times larger, better, and fresher. It is the public relations job of all time. They're super at it. Terribly good at it.

I wonder if it has anything to do with the fact that at one time the English aristocracy was French-speaking.

It's going back a long way, but it may be true. Indeed one would say that for a certain amount of time England was a province of France. Yes, it may well be so.

And America inherits its Gallomania from the English.

Well, they've got it both ways, because if they're simply in a straight line from the British, then yes, they have this pro-French thing, or admiration for the French. If, on the other hand, they're anti-British, then they come to their War of Independence and France was on the right side.

The language of gastronomy interests me. One gastronome writes that a meat soup was so exquisite that he wept at the table; this was followed by a filet of beef that was so tender and succulent that he burst into laughter. Another writes that the venison that he was served was covered with a pink sauce that cloaked it like the mantle of a Byronic poet. Still another writes of a live trout, boiled to death in a large cooking pot, and served with a wine, which, he tells the reader, has the color of partridge-eye. This strikes me as a refinement of cruelty, to write of animals in this vein.

Yes. I agree. It is a refinement of cruelty. It's an attempt to deny that animals are individual persons, which it is obvious to anybody who associates with them that they are. They are individuals just as you and I are individuals and there is no actual reason for denying this. I think there is also an element of hysteria in it. I may be an optimist, but I think I detect guilt because it is *so* baroque.

Do you think that if more and more people become vegetarian, it will usher in a new Golden Age?

No, not of itself. Bernard Shaw pointed out that human vegetarians were often very fierce people, and vegetarian animals also are often quite fierce. No, there is no direct connection. If, however, human beings work it out and decide to renounce violence then, obviously, if you renounce violence against chickens, cows, lambs, etcetera, you likewise renounce it against human beings. And then, yes—if we could all manage it—straight into the Golden Age.

It would appear that as soon as flesh began to be an article of man's diet, the Golden Age was gradually debased into the succeeding ages of silver, bronze and iron. Do you think that this increased consumption of flesh corresponds to the metallic debasement of the ages?

I think in the myth there may be a ghost awareness of this, yes. I think this would come naturally for psychological reasons because if one is an infant, one feeds on nothing but milk, and takes to a flesh diet when one is weaned which, after all, in many societies happens a lot later than ours.

So that we are all lacto-vegetarians, originally.

Yes, originally. I think the myth must be a reflection of infancy—the infancy of the species in the history of man, and so forth.

You point out in Black Ship *that Freud's theory of anal eroticism seems to provide a touchstone for Hesiod's concept of the four great ages: the Golden Age, which gives way to the ages of silver, bronze, and iron. Freud has shown that in the infant's mind there is a relationship between its attitude towards its bodily effluents and childbirth. Do you feel there is a correlation between the Golden Age, when men ate vegetarian food, and the fact that they did not hold their bodily wastes in abhorrence?*

Yes, I think there must be a psychological relationship. And, indeed, the whole recent ecological movement must be an unlearning of these lessons of civilization so that one doesn't necessarily find bodily wastes totally abhorrent—whether one's own, or an animal's, or a sewage plant, or whatever. A lot of social attitudes are being unlearned by present thinking, some of which might, through psychological associations, be useful to us as vegetarians.

Augustine meant it to be disparaging when he wrote, "Inter urinas et faecas nascimur," as did Yeats when he wrote, "For love has pitched his mansion in the place of excrement." They regarded it as a stain upon love that the organs of reproduction and the organs of excretion should overlap, largely I suspect, because the excretory organs expel the remains of dead animals which are foul and virulent. I wonder if it is possible that, as the West becomes increasingly vegetarian, we may cease to have this ambivalence towards our reproductive and excretory systems.

I think this is a general social trend that has happened recently. Shaw also expressed his Puritan point of view that if God had any sense of delicacy he wouldn't have put the excretory and reproductive systems next to each other. But I think that people are gradually overcoming this inhibition, whether or not they are vegetarian.

I think that the social development that is connected with vegetarianism is more of one that is beginning to be aware of violence in itself. A hundred years ago, people used to ask themselves about war: is it a just war? I think now people are more inclined to say that if it's a war at all, it's wrong. At last the repressive force in human beings is beginning to direct itself at violence rather than at sexual behavior. Therefore, one would expect vegetarianism to become more fashionable. Puritans now object to the pornography of violence as well as to the pornography of sex, and though I'm not in favor of censorship or repression of any kind, I do regard it as an advance if humans have come to the conclusion that killing people is rather dirtier than fucking people.

Malcolm Muggeridge

M alcolm Muggeridge touched off his greatest firework in a career that has been a succession of exploding fireworks when, as editor of *Punch* in the late 1950s, he wrote an article in which he stated that the British monarchy was a "royal soap opera" that ought to be scrapped. For this, he was declared *persona non grata* at the British Broadcasting Company, and various newspapers refused to carry his pieces. Muggeridge of course rebounded and was soon back at his post smashing establishment icons, but the incident illustrates Muggeridge's gift for inflaming and outraging the English.

Malcolm Muggeridge was born on March 24, 1903, in Sanderstead, Surrey. His father, Thomas Muggeridge, was an early Fabian, and later a Labor Member of Parliament from Romford, Sussex.

Muggeridge was educated at Selwyn College, Cambridge, in the 1920s and for all his contrariety, he has had the sort of Establishment career that meeker souls only dream about. He was a *sahib*, college teacher, and newspaper editor in India during the British Raj; a top journalist for such papers as the *Manchester Guardian* and *The Daily Telegraph* (for which he was foreign correspondent in Washington, Moscow, Cairo, and Calcutta); a World War II Major in the British Secret Service, operating in East Africa, Italy and France (he was awarded membership in the Legion of Honor and the Croix de Guerre); a book critic for *Esquire* until 1975, and he remains a popular figure on British television.

In the midst of all this activity he has written some of the most elegant English prose of this century. His books include: *The Earnest Atheist: A Life of Samuel Butler; The Thirties; Winter In Moscow* (said to have inspired his close friend George Orwell's vision of totalitarian society in *1984*); and an autobiography (called by the *London Times,* "One of the greatest biographies of our time") *Chronicles of a Wasted Time.*

I note that in your book Jesus Rediscovered, *published in 1969, you mention that you had become a vegetarian, so you have been one for some time. How long has it been?*

Well, I'm very bad at remembering these things, but I would say at least fifteen years.

Are you a lacto-vegetarian?

No, because I eat eggs. I also have milk and cheese. But I keep my own chickens, so that I know that the eggs I eat are from free-range chickens, not battery hens.

When you were nine years old, your family sent you to a Tolstoyan commune in the English Cotswalds to recover from a tubercular complaint. Since this commune was founded on the ethical and religious principles of Tolstoy, who was a vegetarian, I'm wondering if the commune itself was vegetarian.

As far as I remember—my memory is a bit hazy—yes. The prevailing orthodoxy was nonmeat-eating and non-drinking. Of course, it wasn't

Christian, it was Tolstoyan; in fact, probably the people there would have called themselves agnostics.

Was this your first exposure to vegetarianism?

Yes, it was, actually. Although some of my father's friends were vegetarians. You see, my father was an early Fabian, and those people tended to be vegetarian.

I'm told that vegetarian restaurants in Russia are still referred to as "Tolstoyan."

Well, it's interesting that you should say that, because I've done two stints of filming in Russia lately. One was making a film on Tolstoy, and the other on Dostoevsky. And of course it's very difficult to get any vegetarian food at all in Russia, because they are great meat-eaters. I used to try to get an omelette or something; it was very, very difficult. And in order to try and persuade them to make an omelette for me, I would say, "Like Tolstoy!" hoping that this would melt their hearts. But in fact, it didn't.

How did you become a vegetarian?

I initially became a vegetarian for this reason: I have a great hatred for the treatment of animals in what we call factory farms. That, I felt, was one of the most horrible and bestial things, and I was constantly protesting about it. Then, when I protested, somebody would say to me, "Do you eat meat?" And if I said, "yes," then they would say, "Well, how do you know that that isn't made in this way?" And I realized that if I were to remain a meat-eater that I couldn't go on protesting.

So that was the actual impulse. But since then I've come to feel that it does purify one, and I would find it very abhorrent to go back to eating meat. I've found that it has got a spiritual significance, but my initial motive was that—to be able to give a valid answer to that. Exactly the same thing arose actually over drugs.. I gave up smoking and drinking for the same reason. Because I lived and taught in the Middle East when I was a young man, and I know what hashish does to people. There again, people would say, "Do you drink or smoke?" And then I would have to say I did.

Do you feel that becoming a vegetarian has brought you nearer to Christ?

I think that all abstemiousness brings one nearer to Christ, and that any form of self-indulgence separates one. It would be difficult for me to understand how anybody could have a close relationship with Christ who had lived a self-indulgent life. I feel there is a relation and I can quite understand why: for instance, the saints and mystics instinctively adopted an abstemious way of life. I do not like to think—and I *don't* think—that there is anything wicked in eating meat, or drinking, or smoking. But I also think that just as an athlete has to train if he wants to be a runner, so, if you are going to have a spiritual clarity of vision, than you too must train, and part of the training is abstemiousness.

Do you think that Jesus was a vegetarian?

I can't imagine our Lord sitting down to a great meal or anything like that. But still, we don't know that that wasn't so, and again I don't think that there is anything intrinsically wrong in eating meat.

In his book, Erewhon, *Butler satirized the vegetarians by having them convert from vegetarianism back to carnivorism because they began to attribute feelings to vegetables and felt they should be treated as sentient creatures. Do you have any idea why he should have been so hostile toward vegetarians?*

Yes, because I think he reacted very strongly against any form of faddism, or what he would have called faddism, and that he was rigorously trying to be a conventional, hearty man. Possibly to cover up his homosexuality; because he was a homosexual. He was frightened. I think that this feeling of hostility to cranks and eccentrics was partly to cover up the fact that he was frightened of having in himself this very dangerous, in those days, irregularity.

So he must have associated vegetarianism with effeminacy.

Well, with crankiness, with not being the hearty, normal type of person—which is what he wanted to be.

Having read your life of Mother Teresa of Calcutta, Something Beautiful for God, *I'm wondering if she is a vegetarian?*

Now, I have always seen her eating vegetarian food, but that may only have been because of her economy. I think that if she were presented with meat, she would probably eat it. But the food that is offered in her house is vegetarian for economical reasons.

Did you flirt with vegetarianism during your tenure as a college teacher in India?

Yes, I did. I tried to reduce my meat consumption. But I made myself ill by eating only Indian food. But of course, India is the happiest country for a vegetarian, because even on the airplanes and so on, they had a special vegetarian menu. You were never in difficulties in finding vegetarian food.

I am surprised that more Englishmen did not become vegetarians in India during the Raj.

Well you see, most of the sahibs, the English, were cut off from the indigenous population so that it wouldn't have come into their lives. They wouldn't have thought of it really, because in those days the English lived an exclusively western life there. They didn't adjust themselves in any way to Indian food.

Do you think the flesh diet of the English sahibs was a means of setting themselves apart from the vegetarian natives?

You probably remember the episode in Gandhi's autobiography. It's rather interesting from your point of view. He was a young law student in London, and he ate flesh because he thought it would make him strong like the sahibs. That was his motive. And then it made him sick—this meat. And he never tried to eat meat again; he became a very strict vegetarian. I think there is an impulse in human beings to copy those things that seem to make for strength and success. Gandhi's idea in eating meat was that the sahibs had conquered us, and that very few of them can control all of us. The reason must be that they eat meat and we don't. And therefore, he tried to eat it and it made him sick. Of course, he carried his vegetarianism to what Westerners would have regarded as a ruthless extreme, because when the doctors had prescribed meat broth or beef tea for his ailing wife, he wouldn't agree to it.

You don't think he was a dangerous fanatic, or a zealot?

Malcolm Muggeridge 97

Well, I think he could have been. He became a Hindu Nationalist, and did things in relation to that which are not particularly edifying. He was also trying very hard to approach the question of Indian independence in moral rather than power terms.

In a sense, Gandhi was right. Because the sahibs ate flesh, they were more violent and more willing to shed blood than he and his vegetarian compatriots.

Right. And it's probably in reacting against that in himself that he became the great apostle of passive resistance, non-violence, which is a Hindu traditon anyway.

Yes. But I understand he got it through Tolstoy.

Yes. That's where he got it primarily. The formative books of his life, which he recorded somewhere or other, were Tolstoy's works, Ruskin's *Unto This Last,* and *The New Testament.*

Since you met Gandhi, the prime architect of Independence, and exchanged views with him, did you gain the impression that Gandhi felt man can achieve salvation, or paradise on earth by political means?

The interesting thing is, you see, that Gandhi came to realize very quickly on, when all the rioting and the troubles started, that the idea of independence as an end in itself had been mistaken. And he quarreled with Nehru, and separated himself from Nehru and the Congress people, the *Swarajists,* because he considered that they had completely corrupted the idea of independence by seeking political power through it. Now when I was out there not so very long ago, I interviewed Rajagopalachari before he died, the old man who had been the first President. And he said to me, "Gandhi was right, and we were wrong. Gandhi said to us, 'Now that you have achieved independence, have nothing to do with power.'" And Raja-gopalachari said, "We should have done that."

I remember your saying in the second volume of your atuobiography, The Infernal Grove, *that not long before World War II, you saw a buxom German lady wearing a saffron robe and spinning thread at the feet of Tagore. You said that you preferred her in saffron to dirndl. I take your point to be that saffron-robed Germans would have been less susceptible to Hitler.*

Well, it was sort of a joke really. I don't think it should be taken too seriously. But dirndl is a kind of affectation, and saffron is a kind of affectation too. I hate all this self-conscious dressing up.

Well, as more and more Europeans and Americans take to wearing saffron, does this augur well for the West?

I doubt it.

One can consider a vegetarian triumvirate made up of Tolstoy, Gandhi, and Shaw. But one of the things that has puzzled me about Shaw, is why he didn't do more to promote vegetarianism instead of investing his energy in quixotic schemes like redesigning the English alphabet.

Well, I think that's a fair point. But you see Shaw was a very unbalanced man, and I'm not quite clear as to why he was a vegetarian, really. Everything he did had some element of exhibitionism in it. And I also think that he was very frightened of his sexuality. In fact. Sidney Webb, his great friend, told me that he had only once indulged himself. And to some extent, perhaps—and I think this might be so with other people—meat-eating is associated with their sexuality. But with Shaw you could never tell what his motives were.

The Jewish-Christian mystic, Simone Weil, wrote in her essay, Forms of the Implicit Love of God, *"The great trouble in human life is that eating and looking are two different operations . . . ." Do you think that in eating the flesh of animals, rather than being content to admire them, we are confusing the operations of eating and looking?*

I see what she means. I would have to think that over a little more, but I see what she means. This eating is a curious thing. And if we consume something rather than loving it and enjoying its beauty and strength and life, there is something terrible in it. And of course, there is all the business of the *Golden Bough,* and eating the king, and all these things. The Sacrament itself. The whole Sacramental idea that you eat the flesh of Christ and drink his blood. It runs into some very deep philosophical questions.

It's interesting that as you point out in The Infernal Grove, *that during World War II, while the members of the French Government in exile were feasting in the fanciest French restaurants in London, Simone Weil was fasting to death in a sanatarium at Ashford.*

Poor Simone. I think there was this mystical impulse in her. She was very unhappy, because she couldn't go to France and be dropped as an agent for the resistance. But she couldn't seem to understand that, because she looked very much like a Jewess, it would have been fatal for the reserve that she joined. Then of course she did have this illness, *anorexia,* that people have of not being able to eat. And I think the business about wanting to fight for the French was something for her to tell to people to justify her not eating. She was forcibly fed at the hospital, but it didn't save her.

If her fatal fast can be put down to her being ill, doesn't it detract somewhat from the heroism of her gesture?

Well, I don't think so really. I think all things we do in life are mixed. She was deeply distressed that she should be, first of all, in America, and then in England, when so many French people were suffering under the Nazis. And also, she had this belief in suffering—in the worthwhileness of suffering—which can become a sort of morbidity, you know. But it also has great truth in it. That's why the part of Christianity that appealed to her enormously was the Cross, of course.

I understand that you greatly influenced George Orwell while he was writing Animal Farm. *Having reread the book since I became a vegetarian, I now find that it could just as easily be interpreted as an argument against man's inhumanity to animals. Perhaps someday it may be remembered better for its treatment of this theme than for its allegorical references to the Russian Revolution.*

Well, it's quite possible, because that might sink into insignificance. But the question of animals never will. And I profoundly believe that insofar as we are brutal to animals, insofar as we just use animals for our purposes, we are laying ourselves open to the danger that that will be done to us.

The farm depicted in Animal Farm *is a rather benign, old-fashioned farm where the animals are free to pasture. What would Orwell have had to say, I wonder, about the modern factory farm?*

I'm sure it would have disgusted him utterly; he would have loathed it. He loved animals, you know. And I think in some ways he understood them better than he understood human beings. I think his animals in *Animal Farm* are more alive than the characters in his novels. But Orwell was not sympathetic to vegetarians. He regarded them as cranks. And he didn't like cranks.

Have you ever visited the factory farms?

Well, I have seen them. I've seen the chicken ones, which are quite horrifying. And I have put my head in others. But the whole thing nauseates me more than I can tell you. To see meat produced in that way made it impossible for me to eat meat.

Have you ever treated this issue in your essays?

Curiously enough, I have tried to make a parallel between certain types of high-rise housing and factory farms. It's an image that often occurs to me. I think that if men treat animals badly, they will almost certainly treat human beings badly in due course. I remember an old countryman once, when they were doing that myxamatosis business—you know, to kill off rabbits—saying to me, "We shall be punished for this." And in a way we were, because of our pollution and everything. We deliberately slaughtered the rabbits with gas that would produce myxamatosis in them, and now we have made gas to poison ourselves.

Do you think that man is innately violent?

Yes, I think he has violence in him; I don't think that anyone can contradict that. But also, through the grace of God, and to some extent through civilization, he can overcome this propensity.

Do you think that man is innately vegetarian?

Well, I've never been convinced about that. It's quite a controversy, isn't it? I understand that man's biting apparatus is not that associated with a carnivore. But I don't know. However, I think that on the whole man would be living a more natural life if he were a vegetarian.

As a Major in MI5, British Intelligence, during the second World War, you were in Paris during and after its liberation by the allies. It strikes me from your account of Paris in The Victor's Camp, *that the two Parisian establishments that passed through the war virtually unruffled were the elegant restaurants and the couturiers.*

Very largely, Chanel and Maxim's.

Do you have any idea why Paris should be the capital of haute cuisine *as well as* haute couture?

I think because to some extent again what is really meant by "culture" in crude terms is sophistication, isn't it? And a *haute cuisine* is a sophisticated style of eating, and therefore it's thought to go with a cultural sensitivity. I think it is largely an illusion. I suppose it is true that culture flourishes to some extent where there is wealth, and wealth expresses itself in luxuries of various kinds, so culture is associated with luxury. But I think it is a largely accidental association. I mean it is true, if you take Italian cities, their periods of high culture coincided with their periods of commercial prosperity.

The great poets and thinkers of classical antiquity looked back with nostalgia on a Golden Age when humans lived at one with the animals and were vegetarian. Do you think that we will see this Golden Age dawn again?

Well, I can only say that there are few intimations of it in the world at this moment. To me, everything is pointing in the opposite direction—of a relapse into barbarism. I mean, meat-eating, drunkenness, all these different things, really belong to the barbarians. I think that asceticism, self-denial, simplicity of life is really an integral part of a sensitive perception of life, and that you will find gross indulgence, sexual or gastronomic, where this sensitivity is lacking. But where that sensitivity exists, you will find that people tend quite naturally to be very moderate in their indulgences.

Dr. Alan Long

B orn in London on June 5th, 1925, Dr. Alan Long has been a vegetarian since the age of eight. His mother, Kathleen Long, a prominent London pharmacist, devised the cosmetic formulas for the London-based cosmetics firm, Beauty Without Cruelty, whose products contain no animal ingredients, and are never tested on animals. Before she developed the formulas for Beauty Without Cruelty, his mother made up her own beauty preparations on the kitchen stove, and Long remembers that, from time to time, the family would be compelled to take their dinner at a nearby vegetarian restaurant.

Although he attended private schools, Long was a day student who brown-bagged the vegetarian lunches that his mother had fixed for him. Thus the other students were largely unaware that there was a vegetarian in their midst and were given little opportunity for the sort of schoolboy taunting that Long's unusual diet might have otherwise occasioned. Later, at Cambridge, he was a boarding student and was therefore under the necessity of taking his vegetarian meals in the college dining hall in common with all the other members of his college. The meat dishes were so abysmal, however, that Long's vegetarianism, so far from being ridiculed, inspired many converts.

The only place where his vegetarianism got Long into trouble as a youngster was in Sunday School. He would bedevil his teachers with questions such as why the good sheperd was lavished with praise for protecting the lambs from predators, when ultimately it was the good shepherd who would fall upon and devour the lambs in his charge; or, how it was that one could love lambs, and the Lamb of God, and at the same time, love lamb chops. When his questions in Sunday School went unanswered, he stopped attending.

Having had a mother who was a pharmacist, it seems ordained that Long should have become a biochemist. However, during his school and college years, he shone as brightly in his Latin courses as in his Chemistry courses, and it was uncertain whether he would choose to become a Latin professor or a scientist. Science won out. Long took his Ph.D. in Organic Chemistry and Biochemistry from Saint Catherine's College Cambridge, where he specialized in the study of bacterial chemistry and plant germination factors.

In addition to writing a column, "The Long View," for *The New Vegetarian*, he is a research advisor to the Vegetarian Society of the United Kingdom, and a member of its Executive Council. A frequent guest on British radio and television, he is summoned whenever an expert is needed to put the case for vegetarianism.

What caused you to become a vegetarian?

Well, we were interested as a family in animal welfare; my mother worked quite a lot for the Royal Society for the Prevention of Cruelty to Animals, RSPCA, and I suppose I was an inquisitive, inquiring little boy—the scientist was beginning to come out. I began to ask about the fate of the animals, and I began to inquire about the sources of my food, and I discovered to my horror that the lamb, the mutton on my plate, was obtained from the lambs I had seen in the fields. I said, in effect, that I liked lambs and I didn't like lamb, and that was the start of it all.

First of all, I gave up the sort of meats that I didn't like very much, rather fatty meats, and then gave up meat altogether, and chicken, and then fish, so I suppose you could say I went the whole hog.

I owe a lot to my parents, who were understanding and sympathetic; then they too became vegetarians. During the 1939-1945 war, my mother busied herself with the Nature Care Clinic in London, which was—and is—an estimable vegetarian charity trying to reconcile the best in nature cure and orthodox medicine. Her experience of nursing helped at the Clinic. She met some splendid pioneering collaborators: Nina Hosali, George Miller, and Drs. Edward Moore, Valentine Knaggs, and Bertrand Allison, to name a few. "Bertie" Allison's leaflets, which the Vegetarian Society published, were really a set of Dietary Goals, based on the epidemiology he'd carried out as a conscientious doctor years before his time.

Later my mother employed her experience as a pharmacist when she joined Lady Dowding in Beauty Without Cruelty: she produced soaps and cosmetics without ingredients from slaughterhouses. The products were created in our kitchen and tested on animals and ourselves. For a long time our food was scented and perfumed by the natural ingredients accumulated for these endeavors: we boasted that you could eat my mother's cosmetics.

You can see I inherited plenty of reason to think out my ideas.

Does that make you a lacto-vegetarian?

I'm pretty well a vegan, that's a vegetarian who doesn't eat dairy produce. At home I'm almost a vegan; when I'm out, I try to exist like that as much as possible, but I do have to eat out a fair amount, so I have to eat cheese quite a bit. Vegetarians are compromised over dairy produce; in the United Kingdom, where beef and milk are produced in an integrated system, 70 to 80 percent of the beef is reared from calves out of the dairy-herd. The annual British kill of cattle and calves is about 3 million.

Did you find it difficult being a lone vegetarian at school and University?

Yes. At that time we didn't know any other vegetarians, and it was a time, certainly in Britain, when you didn't talk too much about food;

it was not regarded as decorous. The atmosphere has changed quite a lot now, and people are curious about food and different sorts of food. But in those days we didn't know very much; we didn't know a protein from a calorie.

When I went to college, I found some resistance, but I held on; they prepared a vegetarian meal for me and gradually a whole table of vegetarians developed, because some of the Indians, who would otherwise have gone over to eating meat, joined me. The college food was not very good anyway; quite a lot of people became vegetarians more or less as a rebellion against the general standard of poor food, and I'm pleased to say now that my old college actually has a vegetarian table, so a vegetarian meal is always on the menu.

Did you study biochemistry with a view to vindicating your vegetarian diet scientifically?

No, I didn't at that time. I studied science because I was interested in chemistry; it was only later, when I began to see what a good case we had for vegetarianism, that I buckled to and decided I would learn as much as I could so that I would be able scientifically to explain my vegetarianism to other people; more than that, I wanted the facts to persuade them too. Every minute of every working day over 3,000 innocent harmless .animals are slaughtered in the United Kingdom alone. This massacre is an avoidable obscenity I wanted to scout.

Would you classify man as a vegetarian, anatomically and physiologically?

I would say he can be a vegetarian perfectly well, he could be a meat-eater perfectly well. He's adaptable, and the evidence is that he's a nibbler rather than a gorger. And usually, the nibbling animals are more inclined to be vegetarian than the gorgers, which are meat-eaters. We eat several meals a day, and we are equipped to do that perfectly well, so we are nearer the nibbling animals.

We've got to remember, really, that we're living in the agricultural revolution, and if you think of our time on this earth as a thousand-page book, the agricultural revolution has lasted the time equivalent to the last few words in that thousand-page book. So until this very recent agricultural revolution, we've been mainly fruit and nut eaters, hunter-gatherers, with the emphasis more on the gathering than the hunting.

In your opinion, what food substances contain protein in its purest, most nutritious form?

Protein occurs, of course, in all flesh (human flesh and animal flesh), but in the vegetable kingdom, protein occurs abundantly in the pulses, the legumes (beans, peas, lentils, chickpeas), all the items that form a part of the eastern cuisines; we should literally have a bean-feast. There's a lot of protein in cereals. People often forget this; they think that cereals are just carbohydrates and "fattening." The great importance of the vegetable proteins is this: when you combine vege-table proteins from different sources, each one supplements, and complements the other; so they make a very nice balance. Protein is one of the sacred cows of Western nutrition. It's a sacred cow that we in the affluent countries could kill; we are obsessed with protein.

Does man thrive best on a vegetarian diet, do you think?

You can have a poor vegetarian diet; you could live on potatoes all the time, or you could live on cassava as they do in many parts of the tropical belt. That would be a very poor vegetarian diet. But I think you could eat well, enjoy your food on a vegetarian diet, and be very healthy and you'd have something very important apart from the general basic nutrition—you'd have fibrous substances which would control your appetite, so you wouldn't have a tendency to run to fat. Just replacing meat by dairy-produce is not much of an advance; replacing it by cereals and pulses is.

In one of your columns, you cited an article in the Daily Telegraph *which reported that some doctors at Stanford University now believe that a vegetarian diet is among the most healthy diets.*

Yes, nowadays you can hardly open up a medical journal without some new paean of praise to whole grains and nuts, along with increasing doubts about high consumption of animal fats and animal protein. Cancer of the breast, cancer of the gut, cancer of the colon, seem to be associated with high consumption of meats, or animal pro-tein. I think a lot of this has come about because of people taking more of an interest in epidemiology—the study of statistics of human dis-eases. One of the foremost studies of that type was the connection of smoking and lung cancer. They're now pursuing it with dietary habits and beginning to find that vegetarians have been doing the right things: they tend to be breast-feeders, to take a lot of exercise, to eat moderately, not to smoke—or at least not to excess, to drink alcohol in moderation, and, of course not to eat meat. Now, all of those are practices that modern medicine recommends for people to be healthy. I am very happy to be collaborating with doctors and nutritionists in epidemiological studies of groups among the British population.

Still, doctors appear to be extremely backward in nutritional knowledge.

Yes, many doctors are. What you read in the medical journals is very often what most doctors will be saying in ten to fifteen years' time because unfortunately it takes some time to filter through. Many medical schools in the United Kingdom and in the United States are very backward in providing nutritional knowledge, and this has been commented on in these countries. Just recently there were several articles in the *Journal of the American Medical Association* drawing attention to the skimpy education that American doctors get in nutrition. The great populations are only just beginning to get this message; and the increasing consumption of meats and fats and so on is beginning to be halted—as you can see in the various reports of medical and health committees. So orthodox nutritionists and doctors are starting to take much more notice of these trends.

I'm sure you are familiar with the argument against vegetarianism found in Samuel Butler's Erewhon *in which the Erewhonians renounce their vegetarianism when they discover that plants are sentient creatures. What is your answer to this argument?*

Well, I think that possibly in our next incarnation if you believe in reincarnation—I'm an agnostic, by the way—that will be a problem to tackle. I take the view, as the majority of people do, that animals feel fear and pain far more than a plant does. So one should get priorities right and take account of the avoidable cruelties inflicted on animals in markets, on farms, and in slaughterhouses. I would say that the priorities are to begin to relieve the animal kingdom of the dreadful cruelty that's inflicted on it, and to progress. Some laws protect some animals from cruelty and terrorization. At the moment I'm more concerned that farmstock are exempted from even these exiguous protections, for instance, the stockman and slaughterman emasculate—without anesthetics—and kill food-producing animals by methods that would be illegal, at least, in the United Kingdom, if a vet used them to neuter or "put to sleep" a pet.

In addition to being a research consultant to the Vegetarian Society of the United Kingdom, you write a monthly column in the New Vegetarian *magazine in which you report on conditions in slaughterhouses throughout England.*

That's correct. I write on other topics, of course. I like to think through the feasibility and the corollaries of our arguments. The Vegetarian Society's Green Plan, published in 1976, and on which we work all the time, does this. It considers the production and consumption of food and the repercussions on our health, the environment, and the economy. We don't shirk problems such as sources of insulin and heparin, and of vitamin B_{12}. We try to promote developments of plant-meats and plant milks. But all this shouldn't distract us from condemning the slaughtering industry.

What sort of clothing do you wear on your visits to the slaughterhouse?

I usually turn up in my ordinary clothes and I see what they say. From the hygiene point of view, they should make sure that one is wearing clean, white overalls. But very often, they don't take much interest. On the most recent occasion, the foreman said, "Well, you've got something with you to put over your city clothes haven't you, because there's a lot of blood in there." And in fact I had got old clothing, but they made no attempt to see if it was hygienic. For all they had known, I might have been wading around in manure before I went in.

They don't issue a smock, or a protective garment?

No, they don't. They should, but they don't.

Do you have to pass through a reception area before you enter the·slaughterhalls?

No. I had announced that I would like to see the place. I usually get there early, before they start slaughtering, so I can wander around and have a look at the premises.

What time do they start?

The time varies; they usually start fairly early, about eight, or half-past eight. Usually, the small animals are slaughtered first—the calves, and the lambs—what they call the "smalls." They do those first in the morning and first in the afternoon as well. Then they move on to the larger animals.

The animals are delivered to the slaughterhouse in lorries, cattle trucks; they are then herded into the lairage, which is near the slaughterhouse, where they are supposed to be kept quiet; and they wait there until they are driven into the slaughterhouse. They're driven through a passage, through a race, so that each animal comes in singly, rather than in a pack. And they then get driven into what's called a "crush," which is a device for restraining them at one time. There is, say, one line killing cattle, and they'll probably kill about ten or fifteen an hour, and they'll have another line doing the smaller animals—sheeps, lambs, and calves—killing thirty or so animals an hour.

Are they immediately stunned as they enter the crush?

No, they're not always stunned. In Muslim slaughter stunning is not normally practiced although Muslim communities in the United Kingdom are accepting the use of pre-slaughter stunning, provided that the devices aren't used on pigs and that the ritual—the *bismillah* prayer, for instance, which begs Allah's forgiveness for the taking of a life—is observed. In Jewish ritual slaughter, *shechita,* they're not stunned at all. In shechita, the animals are driven into the casting pen, which turns them over; it's arranged so that a man can push it, and then the animal is upside down and it has its throat cut.

If it's stunned, in other methods, what they usually do—in the case of cattle—is to drive the animal into a "shooting box," which is another sort of crush. The animal's head is pushed through an opening. They then take a captive-bolt pistol and fire the bolt into the forehead, it penetrates for a couple of inches, and that should stun the animal. Then it's common British practice to use what's called a "pithing rod," which is driven into the hole opened in the animal's forehead by the captive-bolt pistol, into the brain, and that increases the stunning process.

It doesn't kill the animal; in fact, when the pithing rod is inserted, the animal struggles furiously, but it is actually stunned. You do get a reaction, a sort of Saint Vitus's dance—involuntary movements, presumably. When the animal is stunned, it falls with a great clatter—because it is confined in a metal crush. A door opens at the side, and the body tumbles out. If the animal has been properly stunned, it's got a bewildered look on its face.

Pigs are often stunned with a pair of electric tongs that are placed on either side of their heads, and an electric current is passed through their brains. That should stun them. But the danger with that method is that if it's not properly administered, and the current doesn't pass properly, the pigs are only shocked, that is, they are curarized. They are unable to cry out, but they can still feel pain. Even though they can't struggle or move, they can still feel pain, so that's a very unsatisfactory method.

Electric current often is used for sheep as well. It can't be used on the larger beasts. Hairy sheep should be shorn on their heads before they are "stung," but many slaughterhouses don't boast the shears for the job. Many sheep go "on the rail" conscious; the electrodes are often in poor condition. High technology is hardly in place in a shambles!

When do they actually begin to butcher the animal?

Usually, they hang it up by the hind legs and proceed to cut its throat. With sheep, they lay them out on a table with their heads protruding over the edge of the table, cut their throats, and then leave them to bleed. It takes about five or six minutes before the animals actually die. You hear a sigh as they die; the lungs collapse. Their tongues protrude grotesquely.

During all this time the animals are bleeding, a bullock, for instance, will yield about 3½ gallons of blood before it dies. That's a bucket of blood—a very large bucket. From a cow you get rather more, about 5 gallons. This is done over a "bleeding-pit."

Very quickly, sometimes even before the animal dies, they grab axes and choppers to lop off the horns and start trimming it up. Then they slice it open, right down the middle, and as they slice it open, there is a ripping noise, which sounds like an adhesive bandage being quickly peeled from one's skin. Then all the guts and the intestines spill out; they're still warm, so if it's a relatively cold day, there's a lot of steam billowing up. Then they do what is called "dressing" that is, they tear the hide off—flaying—and after that, they start dismembering the body, pulling out the offals, and what they call the "pluck", which is the lights or lungs, the spleen, the liver, and the heart; these organs are attached to the esophagus and trachea or windpipe, and are hung up on a hook.

Then the carcass begins to take the form that people are accustomed to. The legs are chopped off, or at least the hooves are; these, the workmen usually kick out of the way. As you walk through the slaughterhouse, you often have to kick the hooves aside; it's rather gruesome. A lot of the bits are tossed into bins, where they are kept in case of a medical examination. The bits from each animal are kept separate, so that if anything wrong is found, the whole carcass, if necessary, and all the matching bits can be condemned.

One often sees livers riddled with parasites, called flukes. They look repulsive. The affected bits may be cut out or the whole liver may be condemned. Actually, human consumers of such material would not become infected, but the livers are usually rejected—and used for pet-food—on what the trade calls "esthetic" grounds.

The offals and by–products, which are called the "fifth quarter," really make the difference between make and break for the butcher, because they're very valuable, especially the hides for leather. Then there's the fat; a lot of fat is sloughed off. You have to remember that with a bullock, for example, only about 40 percent of the live weight is saleable meat. The other sixty percent comprises blood—which is sometimes used in food, or dried down and processed into fertilizer, or simply allowed to go down the drain; the tail—which is often used for ox-tail soup; the offals, bones, and the pluck—I think you call them the organmeats in the United States—and the tripes. The intestines, runners, are literally yards long—something like 150 feet for cattle, 104 feet for sheep, and 72 feet for pigs. They are used, for instance, as casings for sausages, as strings for musical instruments and sports racquets, and for pharmaceutical products.

And, of course, the enormous stomach of the ruminant is useless; it is full of what they charmingly call "gut-fill." The gut contains undigested grass at one end to very-much digested grass at the other end, which is manure. However, the slaughterhouses are very far from being 100 percent efficient. Most slaughterhouses don't use the blood. And what they pour into the sewers uses up an enormous amount of oxygen in the sewage works. The slaughterhouses in Britain cause pollution equivalent roughly to a city of nearly three million people.

A great deal of manure is carted away from slaughterhouses. And one of the least desirable jobs in a slaughterhouse falls to the lot of those workers who are charged with the task of going through the offals and cleaning out the tripes. Nowadays, because labor is so expensive, they usually don't do much with the tripes but sell them for pet food. In the old days, they used to turn them inside-out, scrape out the manure, treat them, and then they would emerge as tripes. I think you have tripes in the States, don't you.

They're regarded as something of a delicacy.

Well, of course, a lot of the offals are considered delicacies. In France, particularly, where the cuisine is esteemed, they generally make better use of the offals. Convenience dictates that steaks are prized in Britain and America because they're very easy to cook, actually. You need much more skill to make a tasty dish from some of the offals; a lot of culinary skill lies in the sauces, herbs, and spices used to trick out the meat. But gourmets and connoisseurs set great store by them.

You've said that veal is the dirtiest four-letter word in the vocabulary of meat. Why?

Primarily because of the conditions in which the animals are kept and marketed. Toward the end of their life, when they're about three months old, they're unable to turn around; they're kept in crates. Also they go to slaughter almost as babies; they're very young. These are very cruel circumstances even for a grown-up animal, and for a very young animal it's even worse; so it's about the cruelest part of the whole business. Many slaughtermen detest it. "They should ban it; it's sheer bloody murder," they told me at the last abattoir—a nice euphemistic word, that!—I visited. It's a poignant moment when a bewildered little calf, just torn from its dam, sucks the slaughterman's fingers in the hope of drawing milk and gets the milk of human unkindness. It is a relentless, merciless, remorseless business.

Why isn't it possible to anaesthetize these animals with drugs before they're slaughtered?

It isn't possible to do that for two reasons. First of all, the drugs would be present in the flesh, and so the consumer would become pretty drowsy as well. However, this does happen sometimes with pet foods; they will tranquilize horses before slaughtering them with the result that the dogs and cats, who eat the horses that are ground up in their pet food, are doped. They sometimes dope surplus dairy calves knackered as meat for hunting dogs. But obviously, you can't dope animals who will become food for human beings. Secondly, you don't get a good bleed-out if the animal is drugged. A very important part of producing meat that's acceptable to the modern consumer is to have a vigorous bleed-out; so the animal mustn't be drugged at that time.

You must remember that the fastidiousness really is in the meat-eater rather than the vegetarian. Meat eaters have some funny punctilios; they will quite happily eat cattle, pigs, and sheep, but when it comes to eating horses and dogs and suchlike, they begin to get very squeamish. The whole business is not usually very carefully considered by the average consumer. But it is very important to get meat that is not *too* bloody for him; because if it has got a lot of blood in it, the consumer begins to feel a little queasy about it, and he rejects it because it oozes and putrefies quickly.

Wouldn't a frightened animal bleed faster?

No, it's rather tricky. If the animal has been too frightened, it uses up its glycogen; and after the animal has died, rigor mortis sets in, just as it does with anybody who dies. If you have exhausted the glycogen, there's little to be converted into lactic acid as the process of rigor mortis goes on. That lactic acid makes the meat more acid, which helps to preserve it and prevent it from putrefying. Now if the animal has very little glycogen in its muscles, then it will produce very little lactic acid in the death process, and the meat will be very soft and will putrefy very rapidly. So there's an effort made to see that the animal is not too long struggling about. In most slaughterhouses, they have what are called "lairages" where the animals are fed and watered for a time and kept fairly quiet before they go in to be slaughtered.

What are some of the cruelest aspects of the slaughterhouses?

I've already mentioned some. I'd add the dreadful din and clatter. Because you've got saws rasping and whining; you've got the rails hoisting the animals up; you've got the banging report of the captive-bolt pistol; the clanging of the metal casting-pens; and so on. Animals are very sensitive to noise, and they are terrified of metal clanging. Meat inspectors are now demanding provision of ear-plugs for themselves in slaughterhouses. Also, four-legged animals don't like walking downhill. Yet you often find that somewhere in the slaughterhouse they've got to walk downhill. That always makes them edgy and throws them into a bit of a panic.

And there's all this slaughter going on around them! You've got these wretched animals hanging up on the rail, twitching, as they bleed out. They twitch and kick quite vigorously, which presents quite a hazard to the slaughtermen actually; you can easily get clouted by the back leg of a fair-sized bullock, while it's bleeding out.

It's a very disagreeable atmosphere. You can hardly believe that it belongs to this century. There's not doubt at all that no concession is made at this point for the terror of the animal in its last moments. In Britain animals aren't supposed to see one another being slaughtered, but that rule is very often flouted.

Which is the most inhumane method of slaughter?

I think the most inhumane part is the capsizing of the animal in the ritual slaughter. There is no doubt at all that this is a horrifying process. The animal is terrified; it is struggling for its life: it sometimes nearly struggles out of the cage—in fact, in some instances, it actually manages to escape. In those struggles, it's really a half-ton steer struggling like a little puppy to free itself. It's not a pretty sight at all. And of course the animal bellows. It bangs it head against the floor, or against the walls of the cage. It starts to bleed, and of course there is this blood spattered on the cage for the next animal that comes in.

In the United Kingdom, a thriving Jewish Vegetarian Society attests to the concern of many Jews that all the methods of slaughter are ghastly. Meat slaughtered in this way is not restricted to Kosher butchers; for technical reasons, much of it, as well as the offals and by-products, are sold in the ordinary way.

England has a reputation for having the most humane abattoirs. Is it deserved?

No. It's not deserved. I don't think there is much humanity in any abattoir anywhere. We have cases where the animals are not even rendered insensible when they should be. After they've been stunned, many animals recover consciousness, and then they are struck, that is, they have a knife thrust into them. In a way, they die two deaths. So the English love of animals certainly doesn't penetrate the shambles.

I regret that the cruelty extends to the treatment on the farms, in transit, and at market. You still meet farmers who aver that none of their stock will go for ritual slaughter, but even they quickly lose interest when the farm gate closes behind the animals on their ride to market and slaughterhouse. Few farmers see their animals through the slaughterhouses. To their credit, some farmers refuse to deal in the veal trade and some butchers refuse to sell veal.

How do the slaughtermen behave in the midst of all this?

Well, I play it fairly low key and for some reason they are always very willing to talk to me. Of course I don't tell them that I'm a vegetarian. I manage to fall into conversation with the manager, and during the tea break, I've often gone with the gang of slaughtermen to their hut, when they are all bloody and disheveled from the slaughtering, and had a cozy tea break with them. I try to find out as much as I can and get their point of view. The sort of revealing remark that they'll make is, "Well, it's legal, isn't it?" And I always think that in that remark there is a suggestion that they are perhaps a little bit surprised themselves.

They have a defensive attitude towards their work and I have found that usually they will tell you—particularly as they get older and they can pick and choose a bit—that they are disturbed about the slaughter of lambs and calves. They will say, "Well, they're just babies; I feel a bit of a bugger doing it, because it nuzzles up and it licks my fingers before I stick the knife in." Slaughtermen don't like slaughtering horses, and a lot of slaughtermen have told me that they don't like ritual slaughter.

They have various sentimental quirks. For instance, sometimes a ewe will give birth in the slaughterhouse, and they won't slaughter the lamb; they'll feed it, make a pet of it. But then, there isn't much point in slaughtering a lamb that size because there's hardly any meat in it; it's nearly all bone. So what the slaughtermen do is make a pet of it and then ultimately they give it to a farmer. It comes back a bit later on, unrecognized, and it is slaughtered just like all the others.

Also, occasionally you get what is called the "Judas sheep"—the one sheep that goes along "like a lamb to the slaughter." Many sheep struggle and get anxious and worried, but the Judas sheep will go in undaunted; it will have a soothing effect on the sheep as they are lead in to be slaughtered. Because it has this quietening effect upon the other sheep, the slaughtermen try to keep it as a sort of pet for as long as they can.

Do you think this is a dehumanizing occupation?

Yes, I do. And I think that the consumer is every bit as responsible. I don't feel that one should blame the slaughtermen entirely. It's degrading. I think the consumer is responsible for having this done, and I always say that the last act of the Vegetarian Society should be to rehabilitate the slaughtermen that it has thrown out of work. The community at large should help to find employment for them as well.

In Britain these trades are officially classified as "offensive"; there is a list of offensive trades, and pretty well all the slaughtering jobs come under that category. So that's not just my definition; it's the government's.

All through the business—and I've even heard vets say this—runs the feeling "Well, they're going for slaughter, aren't they?" It excuses cruelty and negligence. Many primitive people associate the periodic culling and emasculations of their herds with orgies. An accompaniment of debauchery is at least in keeping with the activities. An old superstition of slaughtermen held that the presence of a menstruating woman spelt trouble. I wish it had lingered; a few determined vegetarian ladies could quickly bring the places to a standstill!

Have you brought other visitors with you to slaughterhouses?

No, not often. It's not too easy to get a party of people admitted without creating suspicion because as soon as the operators think they're being inspected, they tidy up the practices. When nobody is looking, a lot of things happen that shouldn't. I regret that most people don't want to know much about the transition between bullock and beef. One reporter I took with me fainted when the blood tank overflowed. That put an end to his observations.

What are the hygienic conditions like in the slaughterhouses?

They're improving, but they're pretty dreadful because after all, you have a beast that is full of everything from grass to manure and most of the carcasses are contaminated by bacteria from the feces and urine. You constantly get admonitions from health inspectors and

Dr. Alan Long   117

doctors and so on about the dangers of bacterial carriage in meat.

In fact, and here I quote medical officers of health, one should handle raw meat as if it were cow dung. Wash the hands afterward and don't let it contaminate working surfaces, and certainly, don't let it get near already cooked meat because you get Salmonella, particularly, transmitted from the feces. These bacteria are there by weight in very small amounts but they can cause a lot of trouble, and they also continue to proliferate in the meat as it is stored. What you do normally is to kill off the bacteria by cooking.

The main danger is with raw meat in the kitchen contaminating the cutting board, the refrigerator, the table and so on, so that bacteria are transferred into the cooked meat. Most meat is contaminated. You can't see the contaminations, and ordinary meat inspection would miss all this. In Britain, four out of five cases of food poisoning are caused by meat or meat products—by poultry in particular.

Does cooking succeed in killing the bacteria in meat?

Yes, cooking will kill off most of the danger, but one has to be careful that one thaws out and cooks well any frozen meat—that's very important. It must be thawed out for a good long time. And also, you shouldn't let it cool. down slowly and heat it up slowly. There's a danger in re-heated meat owing to spore-forming bacteria called clostridia, and you can get clostridial food poisoning from reheated meat. Botulism is a form of clostridial food poisoning that may be transmitted even by heated meat and fish.

Is fish contaminated with faecal bacteria as well?

You do get that. Fish, including shellfish, often pick up vibrio bacteria as well as viruses from human populations, because, after all, they may come from polluted water contaminated with human faecal deposits.

Botulism can occur even in vegetable matter, can't it?

It can, yes, because it's carried by soil. Botulism from vegetables has hardly ever occured in the United Kingdom, but cases have been reported in the United States from home bottling and canning. The word, *botulism,* actually is derived from the Latin for "sausage".

Today sausages are treated with preservatives; like nitrites and sulfites to prevent botulism; however, the nitrites themselves have got hazards associated with them because they generate nitrosamines, which are carcinogenic. So you don't often hear of botulism these days because the most suspect meat is treated with these additives, which are far from ideal. The normal sort of food-poisoning organisms that one gets cause relatively low toxicity but nonetheless they will cause illness of several days duration, and death among older people and very young children who may get bacterially caused disease by communication from adults who have eaten contaminated meat but are free of symptoms. Of course, a lot of ailments caused by meat are not properly diagnosed. You get things like summer colds, and upset stomach, and Montezuma's Revenge, Delhi Belly, the Aztec Two-step, which are usually bacterial food poisoning, and usually caused by meat—certainly by temperate climates.

One of the biggest advantages of being a vegetarian, aside from the health benefits, is the fact that one can contemplate the whole process of producing one's food right from the seed to the table to the mouth with no demur; whereas meat-eaters would not be very happy to contemplate the slaughterhouse process necessary in the preparation of their food. It is very curious how people will dwell on their wine, and talk about it in the minutest detail, but they certainly wouldn't like to dwell upon the origins of the meat. Many couldn't tell you if their steak came from a cow, a steer, or a bull, or whether the best was a Hereford, an Angus, or a Friesian. They don't expatiate on the connection between bleed-out and tenderness.

Why would anyone wish to eat so potentially dangerous a substance? Do you think flesh is a status food?

Yes, it's acquired a status; it's thought that a high consumption of meat is synonymous with a high standard of living, and possibly with virility. It's a meretricious high standard of living, and it's got nothing to do with the quality of life. But a high consumption of meat, a high consumption of dairy food, and a high consumption of refined food are regarded as the prerequisites of a high standard of living.

But that trend is being reversed; it's now the rich people who send out for brown bread. It's rather the superior thing now to eat a lot of vegetables and fruit, and it's the poorer people in the affluent nations who eat the refined foods and sugary abominations. So we're having a swing right the other way over. After all, steaks are only textured vegetable protein hacked out of a bullock's backside. That flawed symbol of virility is the flesh of the eunuch, with some further hormonal tinkering administered by the farmer doctoring the feed. Farmer Giles is no more; now it is Pharmacist Giles.

It's not yet a mass movement, but vegetarianism is becoming trendy. It's no longer *outre*. It goes with ecology and conservation, and people who are worried about the world food problem. It's reinforced by the argument that it's very wasteful to produce feed rather than food; in other words, feeding animals to produce flesh food is a monstrous inefficiency at a time when millions of people are starving for actual food.

It seems ironic that man should choose to eat carrion. Man must rate himself the most ruthless predator. It's funny that the expression "to behave like animals" is always regarded as representing reprehensible behavior, for in many ways the animals behave much *better* than we do. They have territorial battles, but very often these are conducted without the bloodshed that accompanies disputes of this kind among humans. They go through a ritual, and once they're finished, they don't seem to entertain hatred. Maybe they're not as intelligent as we are and they're not as clever, but at least they don't hate. To that extent, it could be regarded that "to behave like the animals" should be construed as a compliment. Would that the overweening cleverness of our species were tempered by the qualities of humility and mercy. Live and let live, I say.

Do you think that the slaughtering of animals contributes to the callousness of humanity?

Obviously, if you accept without demur the slaughtering of animals, you can accept the slaughter of your own kind. The Indian religion is very much based on the policy of *ahimsa,* which is a pacifist policy. The Western religions are rather more materialistic and are equivocal, particularly over the slaughtering of animals. And where they are pretty clear on this topic, it seems they're ignored. Isaiah said that "He who killeth an ox is as if he slew a man." There doesn't seem to be much doubt about that; it's unequivocal and unambiguous, but that teaching seems to be fairly widely flouted. If one is callous in any way, even if it's to a plant, or to the earth, one will be callous to human beings.

Do you think that if more and more people become vegetarian, it will usher in a new Golden Age?

I don't think we must be too heady about his. But I think the world is getting better, and that we may perhaps be on the threshold of a silver age. We could strive for the gold. It requires us to recognize our frequent resort to ruthlessness to our fellows and to other forms of life.

I think the time will come when the word *vegetarian* will be taken as routine and will become superfluous. We're advancing to the point when you won't ask if anyone is a vegetarian. Most of the people will be vegetarian. When you come to interview someone for the book in your next incarnation, you'll come to a little office like this and find people who will be hunters, maybe, and they'll possibly be grilling a steak. And they'll hark back to days when meat-eaters were preponderant—and they'll be a minority. People will have a special word for them just as we reserve one for cannibals; they'll be called "meat-eaters," a rather funny, gruesome people. I think vegetarianism will just slide in, and meat-eating will be regarded as an unfortunate aberration.

Dr. Gordon Latto

A s the president of both the Vegetarian Society of the United
Kingdom and the International Vegetarian Union, Dr. Latto is
that anomaly, a vegetarian physician, as are his wife Barbara (a nutritionist); his sister-in-law, Monica (a general practitioner); his
younger brother, Douglas (a gynecologist and obstetrician); and his
younger brother, Conrad (a surgeon).

Born in Scotland on June 25th, 1911, the eldest of four sons,
Latto qualified in medicine at Saint Andrews University. Since there
were no courses in nutrition in his medical curriculum—a deficiency
that still exists in medical schools—Latto felt compelled to travel to
various spas and clinics, such as the Bircher-Benner Institute in

Switzerland, in order to learn the nutritional methods of healing that his university medical training had omitted.

In his younger days, Latto was a top amateur golfer whose victories at golfing competitions helped to persuade people that vegetarians were not physical weaklings. He was also a keen long-distance walker, routinely walking up to a hundred miles or more. (Recently, a party of his vegetarian friends walked a distance of some 300 miles in ten days—from Goteborg to Stockholm—on a diet of nothing but water.)

A vegetarian diet, Latto believes, promotes endurance. One of his former patients—who under Latto's guidance became a vegetarian by preference—was the late Sir Frances Chichester who, in 1967, sailing a 53 foot ketch, the "Gipsy Moth IV," became the first man to circumnavigate the world in a solo voyage. Writing in a June, 1968, article for *Esquire*, ("Keeping Fit With Sir Francis Chichester"), Sir Francis credits Dr. Latto with having cured him of gallstones by means of a vegetarian regimen. It is worth quoting a brief passage from the article:

> I lost my health and the gallstone trouble returned. A doctor, urgently summoned, wanted to operate at once, but once again my wife was convinced that this would be the wrong thing to do. It was then that I met Dr. Gordon Latto, who had become so impressed by the efficacy of nature cure methods that he had switched over almost completely from his orthodox practice to natural healing. He said that he could stop the gallstone from forming, but that I must go on a strict vegetarian diet for a year, besides knocking off drink and tobacco (which he said was worse than drink). This was a tough regime; the gallstones could not survive it. I did, however, and at the end of the period I found that I was also cured of smoking, and that the vegetarian diet suited me so well that I have preferred it ever since.

Sir Francis Chichester is but one of many patients for whom Latto's vegetarian regimes have produced remarkable cures. Despite the number of patients he must treat, Dr. Latto still finds time to serve as president of the two vegetarian societies mentioned above and to lecture on the salutary benefits of a vegetarian diet all over England and Europe—testimony in itself to the stamina that such a diet provides.

Perhaps we could begin by talking about your background.

Well, I came from Dundee, Scotland. My father was a lawyer, and he wanted me to study medicine, which I did. He became a vegetarian himself when I was about ten years of age. In those days we did what our parents told us, so I became a vegetarian, too. Then, when I left school and went to the university, they challenged me right, left, and center about the scientific aspect of vegetarianism—about which I knew nothing. And I felt, well, it's either scientific or it's not.

So I read about various aspects of vegetarianism—the scientific aspect, the humane aspect, the ethical aspect, and the economic aspect. The more I studied, the more convinced I became that it was a logical procedure, that it would help humanity, that it would lessen the suffering of the animals, and that it would help this country [Great Britain] particularly because the economy in this country is appalling. Fully 85 percent of all the arable and pastoral land in this country is used to feed animals or to grow food with which to feed animals. We import food from abroad to feed animals quite apart from this 85 percent of our own land upon which we are getting such a poor return. That, I think, is unscientific. No wonder the economy is bad! For every 10 tons of protein that is fed to animals, when the animals are consumed subsequently, only one ton is returned. That is an appalling economy. And this nation is in a perilous state economically.

We are very, very cramped in this country, and we utilize our land badly, which is tragic. We have pasturage rather than tillage here. You see, pasturage doesn't give enough people, work; it drives people off the land, whereas tillage employs far more people. With so much of the land in England taken up with pasturage, we are spending millions of pounds every day importing food from abroad. We're ruining the economy and weakening the land. It's a bad, bad system.

Do you think that the western dietary system lays too much emphasis on the consumption of protein?

Definitely. Flesh food is a very concentrated protein, and in order to be utilized, protein has to be broken down into polypeptones and into amino acids. I'll give you an analogy. We are sitting in my house in Reading, England. If we wanted to move this house to London, we would have to take it all down and take the bricks out one by one. But in the process, we would do a lot of damage, and much useless material would be discarded and eliminated. That's what happens when you eat complex protein; there is a lot of material that is wasted and cannot be utilized again.

The bulk of the people take far too much protein. The amount of protein we need is very small. Take the pattern of growth in the baby. Never in your life do you grow as fast as you do in the first six months of your life. You grow from, say, seven pounds to fourteen in six months. Assuming that your mother is feeding you during that period, you are living on mother's milk, and mother's milk has 1.5 percent protein. And the bulk of the people are eating far, far more than 1.5 percent protein in their diet. Even vegetarians tend to take too much protein in the West. If they reduced their protein intake, they would feel better and be better for it. I'm convinced that overconsumption of protein is one of the great problems in the West.

Why do you suppose there has been this overemphasis on protein?

Well, because protein is considered to be essential, and it is essential, but it's the *right quantity* of protein that's essential. If you're a vegetarian, you've got to get a balanced protein. For example, if you take nothing but grains, such as wheat, you're short of lysine—an amino acid; if you take nothing but beans, you're short of methionine—an amino acid. But if you take beans and grains together, you can obtain a perfect protein. Through the ages, people have known that when two proteins that are classified as incomplete are wed together, they produce a complete protein.

That's one of the troubles in India; people tend to live largely on white rice. Some, however, eat pulses (legumes) as well, and pulses and rice are a good combination.

How does the vegetarian Hindu compare with the average Westerner physically?

Well, I would say poorly. In the first place, the Indians, the bulk of them, are underfed. If you're impoverished, of course, you can't expect to be eating well. And the sanitary conditions are ghastly—animal droppings and flies all over the place. No wonder there is so much disease, blindness, and leprosy there.

Many meat-eating Westerners point to India as an object lesson of what can happen to a vegetarian nation.

I think that it's not because of the vegetarianism; it's because the external conditions, the misgovernment, the poverty, the squalor have conspired to give them a bad form of vegetarianism. They eat white bread, white rice, white flour, and a lot of food that shouldn't be eaten which they treat with spices to make it possible to eat. On the whole, the Indian diet is a very impoverished one. But in certain hilly parts of India, the diet is excellent. The Hunza people, for example, have a wonderful diet.

Do you think that originally humankind was vegetarian?

Well, Linnaeus, a very notable son of Sweden, divided animals into various groups, and he placed man in the mammalian group—that in which the mothers suckle the young. And he divided the mammals into four sections: the carnivorous mammal (such as the lion and the tiger) which derives its food from the flesh of animals; the herbivorous mammal (such as the horse) which derives its food from grass; the omnivorous mammal (such as the bear) which derives its food from the animal and plant kingdom; and the "anthropomorphic" primates (such as the baboon). If you compare these four categories, you will find that the carnivorous mammal can only move its jaw up and down, and its saliva is strongly acid. The herbivorous mammal can move its jaws fundamentally in three directions, and its saliva is alkaline; the omnivorous mammal moves its jaws up and down only, and its saliva is acid; and the anthropomorphic primate has a dental morphology and a saliva identical with that of man—it moves its jaws in three directions and its saliva is alkaline.

The carnivorous mammal has great cuspid teeth whereas man does not; the molar and premolar teeth interdigitate, whereas in the case of the herbivorous mammal, you have the molar and premolar teeth tuberculated: like man's. In the case of the omnivorous mammal, concerning the molar and premolar, you have a blunt tooth, a sharp tooth, a blunt tooth, a sharp tooth—showing that they were destined to deal both with flesh foods from the animal kingdom and foods from the vegetable kingdom.

The intestines of a carnivorous mammal are two to five times the length of the body; of the herbivorous mammal, twenty-eight times the length of the body. The omnivorous mammal and the frugivorous mammal, along with man, have intestines that are ten times the length of the body. Carnivorous mammals and omnivorous mammals cannot perspire except at the extremity of the limbs and the tip of the nose; man perspires all over the body. Finally, our instincts: the carnivorous mammal (which first of all has claws and canine teeth) is capable of tearing flesh asunder, whereas man only partakes of flesh foods after they have been camouflaged by cooking and by condiments.

As a medical authority could you say something about the condition of meat today?

Meat consumption has risen enormously in recent times simply because of artificial insemination and the importing of foods from abroad; the amount of meat that is eaten now has quadrupled since the beginning of the century, and the meat is definitely deteriorating from a dietetic point of view.

In the olden days meat wasn't a good food, in my opinion, but meat today is an even worse food, because so many of these animals now are treated with antibiotics to prevent them from getting various infectious diseases, and they are treated with steroids to make them grow more quickly, with the result that when meat from the animals is eaten, you are taking into the system abnormal hormones and antibiotics. I believe that one of the causes of the rise of these endocrine diseases today may well be due to the fact that we are taking so many extraordinary hormones into our system. And, of course, if you take a lot of antibiotics into your system, you'll find that it upsets the colon and causes all sorts of internal problems.

Also, many of these animals are put into confined spaces: take the battery hen. It doesn't range; it remains in a confined space for the duration of its life; it remains there until it is no longer an efficient egg-laying machine, then it is taken out and killed. Pigs are confined as are calves in factory farming. Activity is the law of life. If you don't have activity, you can't be healthy. Therefore, these animals cannot truly be healthy. If you take the flesh from these animals, you cannot be taking a flesh that is fundamentally healthy.

One argument that is urged in favor of meat-eating is that people who live in northern climates require a flesh diet to sustain themselves through the harsh winters.

Well, the great cultures, the great religions, have originated in the warmer climates: India, Persia, Egypt, Hinduism, Buddhism,

Zoroastrianism, etcetera. These were great, great cultures, civilizations and religions long before those of the Northern Europeans were dominant. But gradually man migrated from these Southern regions into the Northern climatic regions, and then he made a great mistake. He started to cook all his foods, so that nowadays his cultural heirs are virtually cooking everything they eat. Eating so many cooked foods is injurious to the health. The true pattern is mother's milk; mother's milk is uncooked. I think this is one of the troubles in the West today—people don't have enough raw food, and they take it in the wrong way. Our continental cousins take their raw food at the beginning of the meal, which is right; in England, they tend to take their raw food at the end, which is wrong.

At his institute in Switzerland, Bircher-Benner (the inventor of Bircher Meusli) would give people as a first course a dish of fruit, then an enormous salad, and then some cooked food at the end; by the time you've come to that, you have eaten so much of the other that you're not interested in it. And he obtained such amazing results from these raw foods. Due to a lack of raw food people used to get scurvy in Europe, especially sailors.

How do you think man initially lapsed from his innate vegetarianism?

That I don't understand at all. Man instinctively is not carnivorous. As I said before, he takes the flesh food after somebody else has killed it, and after it has been cooked and camouflaged with certain condiments. Whereas to pick an apple off a tree or eat some grain or a carrot is a natural thing to do: people enjoy doing it; they don't feel disturbed by it. But to see these animals being slaughtered does affect people; it offends them. Even the toughest of people are affected by the sights in the slaughterhouse.

I remember taking some medical students into a slaughterhouse. They were about as hardened people as you could meet. After seeing the animals slaughtered that day in the slaughterhouse, not one of them could eat the meat that evening.

Also, while we were in the slaughterhouse, the time of the midday break came along; the men were sitting in a square, out in the open in the sunshine, on little benches, eating their meal. One little sheep jumped out of its pen and came over to the men. One of the men was holding a sandwich with a bit of lettuce dangling out of it, and the sheep came and nibbled the lettuce. The man was so amazed to see the sheep eating his lettuce that he handed it another bit of lettuce, and so it went on, and others gave lettuce to the sheep. And when it came to the time for the killing, they would not kill that sheep.

In these slaughterhouses you see violence, brutality, bloodshed, and death—so little love and compassion and pity. What I should like to see is a minimum of animal suffering, a minimum of human suffering. We should help to make this world a more Edenic place.

No flocks that range the valley free
To slaughter I condemn
Taught by a power that pities me
I learned to pity them.

That's from Goldsmith. Ovid also wrote a beautiful poem on vegetarianism. Of course, Percy Bysshe Shelley, who was probably the king of all poets, wrote some wonderful works about vegetarianism, and it was through his wonderful poems that so many people have been influenced.

Never again may blood of bird or beast
Stain with its venomous stream a human feast!

I think that there is something unlovely about the slaughtering of animals. Poets tend to have an exalted vision; therefore they turn away from things that are unlovely, and they turn away from flesh food.

How did it happen that you began to incorporate vegetarian principles in your medical practice?

Well, after I qualified in medicine, I taught anatomy at the university, and then I worked in a country practice. I was studying to take my fellowship when the war broke out and I had to give it up. After the war, I started a practice using diet as one of the main methods of treatment. Hippocrates, the father of medicine, said, "Our medicine should be our food, and our food should be our medicine," and that's more or less the philosophy that I follow. It's amazing what you can accomplish with dietetics.

I think it's a pity that nutrition is not studied in medical schools. You see, I went through the whole of my medical curriculum with never a lesson on nutrition. We all heard about diseases and the drugs to use in treating them. But it's amazing what certain foods can do. Hippocrates himself obtained wonderful results with certain nervous disorders from sprouting grains—marvelous results.

Now there is a big institute in Boston, the Hippocrates Institute, run by Dr. Ann Wigmore, which also treats all sorts of nerve conditions—and other conditions, too—with sprouting grains, with results that are surprisingly good.

But it would seem that most doctors want to treat diseases with the knife rather than the fork.

Well, I think you've got to remember that we are living in a materialistic world. If doctors tell patients that they must change their rhythm of living, and abstain from eating certain harmful foods, people will not want to pay them for that. Whereas if a patient comes along with a grumbling appendix, and the doctor takes out the appendix, the patient is quite prepared to pay a big fee. The symptom has been treated, whereas we should treat the cause.

Why do you think more doctors haven't championed the cause of vegetarianism?

It's very hard work, you know. You may have to speak to a patient for hours before he will consider it.

Who were some of your models as you began exploring vegetarian medicine?

There was one outstanding vegetarian doctor, Anna Kingsford, who was one of the early lady doctors; she qualified in medicine in Paris in 1881. She wrote two remarkable books on vegetarianism. One was called *The Perfect Way in Diet,* this was an English translation of the thesis that she submitted for her medical degree, and the other, which she wrote in collaboration with Edward Maitland, was called *Addresses and Essays on Vegetarianism.* Both are wonderful books.

In our world, the vegetarian world, Anna Bonus Kingsford had a profound influence. The books that she wrote were masterpieces. Of course, they are long out of print, but we've got them in our archives in London. It's a tragedy that they have been neglected. They are wonderful reading; once you pick them up, you can't put them down.

Does the English medical profession look on vegetarian doctors as cranks?

Jesus was looked upon as a crank in his day; Semmelweis was looked upon as a crank in his day; Bircher-Benner was looked upon as a crank in his day. I don't think it matters what people think about you;

I think you have to do what you intuitively feel is right.

Do you always prescribe a vegetarian regimen for your patients?

I do if it warrants it. If a person came in with a lacerated head, I don't think that I would always go the length of recommending it there; but if they came in with some real illness and we talked it over, I certainly would recommend a vegetarian diet. Of course, you mustn't force people to do anything; you've got to show what can be done and what the results are, and try to keep cheerful and well yourself. It's amazing how many people can be positively influenced.

Are more doctors coming over to vegetarianism these days?

Well, the whole nation is moving towards the vegetarian way of living and more and more doctors every year are becoming vegetarian. A surprising number of people are becoming vegetarian, and it's very encouraging to see the way it's growing. Young people in particular are becoming disillusioned with the power of medical drugs and aware of the iatrogenic diseases. And the results obtained from vegetarian regimes in conjunction with other healing techniques—such as breathing exercises, positive thinking, and exercise—are extraordinarily good.

You see, the problem is that people are not getting so much exercise as they used to; they used to walk great distances and run about. Now we're all lounging in motor cars, riding elevators and escalators instead of climbing stairs, and reclining in front of the television. I think that the lack of exercise, the lack of fresh air—because exercise makes you breathe more deeply—and the wrong type of foods—such as flesh foods, white sugar and white rice—are enough to devitalize anyone.

Flesh, white flour, and white sugar were highly prized by the aristocracy in the Middle Ages. Do you think that the popularity of these foods today can be attributed to the desire of people lower down in the social scale to emulate those above them?

Yes, I would say that was true. I think the so-called upper-classes have set a very bad example in eating food like that. You see, members of the upper-classes don't have the problems that ordinary people do. Lots of them have plenty of time for recreation—hunting, riding, golfing, tennis, polo—where they can burn up these foods. Whereas the poorer people may be working in an office all day, and then they come home and eat this type of food which their systems cannot tolerate and ultimately they become ill. There's an enormous amount of illness in this country. I think that people want to improve themselves in every respect, and they imagine that by partaking of these foods that they will improve themselves. Ironically, though, by taking these foods, they are really hurting themselves.

I think it was your fellow countryman, Adam Smith, who observed that from birth, everyone seeks to improve his lot in society. It seems to be a genetic urge.

That's true. Everyone wants to better himself, and I think that is true and proper and right.

I wish I could say that the health of the nation was improving. But look at the amount of drugs that are taken today. When insulin was discovered in 1922, there were about 2,000 diabetics in this country; nowadays—we're supposed to be making progress—we have 500,000 diabetics in this country. Rheumatic diseases, which I think are largely due to rich foods, are increasing; mental diseases are rising; diverticulitis is increasing; coronary diseases are increasing; cancer of the colon has risen dramatically, largely due to the fact that there is so much stasis in the colon; also, cancer of the lung has increased. I don't think you can say that the poor state of health prevalent today is due to meat alone, or to any one thing alone. I think it's a multi-factorial effect, a combination. But I think flesh foods play a very important part.

Our eating habits have changed dramatically since the beginning of this century. For instance, in 1914 the amount of white sugar consumed in this country was ¼ pound per head per week; today it is 2½ pounds. That is a dreadful state of affairs—we consume ten times as much white sugar now! And I think that white sugar is one of the most harmful foods to take. Also, in those days, the amount of roughage eaten in the diet was high; today most foods are refined. We used to have wholemeal breads; today one largely sees white bread and white rice. Eijkman in Batavia fed his chickens on white rice in order to raise prize chickens, but they gradually became ill, so he threw them some brown rice and within a very short time they recovered; it was the vitamin B on the outside of the rice that brought about the recovery. This was only discovered in 1897.

Another interesting phenomenon occurred in Switzerland. There were two groups in a Swiss Valley: one was German Swiss and the other was French Swiss. The German Swiss used to cook their vegetables and throw their water away. The French Swiss used to cook their vegetables, keep the water, and make it into soup. The German Swiss developed goiters, and the French Swiss didn't. That little bit of extra iodine retained in the diet made all the difference between bad health and good health.

There was also another experiment that was rather intriguing, where ostriches were being fed on what appeared to be the correct diet, but they became ill. Then sand was mixed with the diet; the ostriches ate that and recovered, and they remained well. The ostriches' stools were examined, and all the sand that had been mingled with their food came out. We do need a certain amount of roughage in the diet to stimulate intestinal flow. Without roughage, the intestinal transmit times are very slow and the movements are very, very sluggish; whereas when you take roughage, you get a quicker intestinal transit time and more bulky motion.

Vegetarian food passes through rather quickly, does it not?

Fruit and vegetables do tend to pass through quickly. And diverticulitis, a disease of the colon, is very much less manifest in vegetarians than in their meat-eating compatriots.

Where did you get your training in dietetics?

I studied dietetics under a man in Edinburgh, Dr. Gold; then I travelled to Sweden and worked in the Waerland Institute. Waerland was one of the pioneers in Sweden on food reform and vegetarianism. He wasn't a doctor, but he was a very great pioneer in his way of living. There's a very famous bread that he popularized, called the Waerland Bread or Brot. He had institutes in Sweden and some in Germany as well. Then I studied at the Bircher-Benner Institute in Zurich.

Do you basically treat people according to Bircher-Benner's principles?

Well, I do a broader spectrum. His approach was largely diet. I recommend diet very strongly, but I do so many other things as well:

simple herbal teas, breathing exercises, relaxation, exercise, positive thinking—all these come into the picture.

Besides being a practicing physician, you are also president of both the Vegetarian Society of the United Kingdom and the International Vegetarian Union. Could you briefly sketch the background of these groups?

The Vegetarian Society began in England in 1847 in Manchester. And then in 1888 there was a vegetarian society formed in London. And the London Society, the child, grew bigger than the parent; and ultimately the two united in 1969.

In order to celebrate the formation of the vegetarian movement in 1847, at the Diamond Jubilee in 1907, it was decided to unite and form an international vegetarian union; this took place in the following year, in 1908. At that meeting there were about twenty-three people. It took place in Dresden; and since then we have had meetings in different countries to promote vegetarianism. And we have had various presidents whose nationalities have been as international as the countries in which the congresses have been held.

At the congresses, delegates come together and they discuss how they in their nation run their society and what the results are. Each one listens to the other, and then we will pick out the best from each nation and try to incorporate it into a system. We've found that these conferences have been very helpful. There have been great friendships made; we've got very good friends in various parts of the world. And there is a tremendous correspondence going on to see if we can further this movement which we feel would help so much.

In classical antiquity, many of the great poets and philosophers looked back with infinite nostalgia to a Golden Age in which humans were innocent of war and lived in harmony with animals, on a vegetarian diet. Do you think that the vegetarianism that seems to be spreading throughout the world, will usher in a new Golden Age?

I hope it will usher in a *better* age. I could probably answer that question best by quoting a passage from the speech I gave to the 24th International Vegetarian Congress, in India, in the fall of 1977.

"If we harden our hearts to the suffering of the creatures, we must by an immutable law harden our hearts to our brother and sister, and this can never lead to ideal conditions. The adoption of this vegetarian way of life, if the food is balanced, will lead to a new, better, higher, and more noble rhythm of living."

Muriel, the Lady Dowding

Muriel the Lady Dowding was born in London. As a young woman, she met and married her first husband, Max Whiting, by whom she had a son. At the beginning of World War II, Whiting joined the R.A.F. and during his third mission in a Lancaster bomber, he was killed. In her revulsion against the death of her husband and the carnage of the war, she decided that she and her young son would no longer eat animals.

Several years after the war, Muriel met and married Lord Dowding, the man who, as Air Chief Marshal Lord Dowding, had played a major part in saving England from the Nazi onslaught. He had successfully commanded "The Battle of Britain," which many historians regard as the turning point of the war against Germany. Through his wife, Lord Dowding came to know and respect the animal liberation movement, and he, too, became a vegetarian.

As a member of the House of Lords, and as one of the great military figures of World War II, Lord Dowding lent enormous prestige and stature to the animal liberation movement—which could not be taken lightly with one of Britian's heros at its head. His stirring speeches in the House of Lords in aid of the Humane Slaughter Bill culminated in legislation that eased the suffering of animals. The legislation in which Lord and Lady Dowding took the greatest pride was the Protection of Animals (Anaesthetics) Act, 1964, which made it a criminal offense to castrate or otherwise cut into the living flesh of an animal without the use of anaesthesia.

In 1959, Lady Dowding founded Beauty Without Cruelty, an organization that works for the elimination of animal ingredients in cosmetics and the abolition of animal testing in the cosmetics industry as well as discouraging the wearing of animal skins. To this end, it produces its own cruelty-free cosmetics, and markets its own line of simulated furs and leathers. In addition to publishing a quarterly journal, *Compassion,* which reports on the plight of animals throughout the world, Beauty Without Cruelty also puts out a pamphlet called *More Than Skin Deep* that lists which commercial beauty products contain animal ingredients and which do not.

Besides acting as Chairman of Beauty Without Cruelty, Lady Dowding helps to administer The Air Chief Marshal Lord Dowding Fund for Humane Research, which funds the development of alternatives for the use of animals in laboratory tests, and watches over the Dowding Memorial Trust, which provides a sanctuary for abandoned pets in which the animals are free to roam about instead of being caged in kennels. She is also President of the National Animal Rescue Kennels and the National Anti-Vivisection Society—defensive bulwarks against man's inhuman, unceasing war against the animal kingdom.

Historians of the Second World War have said that Lord Dowding was treated rather shabbily after he had won the Battle of Britain. Do you suppose the position he took up in favor of vegetarianism and anti-vivisection had anything to do with this?

Well, undoubtedly it didn't add to his military reputation in the eyes of the powers that be at that time. Nor did it add to his military luster that he studied life after death. He did this entirely because he had so many mothers and war-widows and people writing him. So he wrote a book called *Many Mansions,* which brought help and comfort to many people.

He did it out of compassion, the same motive which led him to investigate the conditions in the slaughterhouses.

Yes. He never cared what people thought about him.

Some people might think it odd that a military man such as your husband should have converted to vegetarianism and become a militant anti-vivisectionist.

My husband was a very compassionate man. When we married, I don't think that this was a side of his life that he had either the time or the knowledge to develop. You see, during the early years of our marriage I was a vegetarian, but I made no attempt to convert him. He was a very healthy man with a very small appetite, very alert in every way. But when we had been married about two years, I said to him, "Do you find it very inconvenient at these big functions having a vegetarian wife?" And he said, "Oh, not at all. I sometimes wonder whether you are fifty years or a hundred years ahead of your time." This of course was twenty-five years or so ago, you see, when there weren't so many vegetarians in England. There are a lot now. And then one day I said to him, "Well, as you eat meat, as you are a peer and have a seat in the House of Lords, could you do something about getting it humanely killed?" He said, "Well, isn't it?" I said, "I'm asking you."

Well, we had a very, very happy marriage, and he never went anywhere without telling me where he was going. He'd nearly always say, "Look, can't you get out of what you are doing and come too?" And on three occasions he didn't tell me where he was going, he had just gone. He came back very depressed and didn't seem to want to talk about whatever it was. I wondered what was worrying him. When Sunday came, his usual salted beef was served, a dish that he liked very much. And he stood up to carve it, then he sat down, and he said, "What is it you're eating?" "Oh," I said, "well, as you know, it's a vegetarian dish." He said, "Would you have enough for me to have some? And don't ever get meat in this house for me again!" And he became a vegetarian then and there, and was one for about seventeen years till his death.

So in other words he must have inspected the slaughterhouse.

Yes, he had. Well, if you're going to speak in the House of Lords, you've jolly well got to know your facts. Yes, he'd been to three slaughterhouses and was appalled. After that, he was able to bring in the Humane Killer for the smaller animals like sheep. At that time it was only used on the oxen and the bigger animals. And later he was able not to ban ritual slaughter, but to mollify it slightly. We met the Imam of Woking Mosque, and he would have been very cooperative about it, because he said, "We believe our God is a God of understanding, and if it should violate the law of the land to kill animals in this way, then we would just say, well, God will understand." But we came up against difficulties with the Jewish fraternity; they felt that this was being anti-Jewish or something. It wasn't at all; it was merely being humane. So he was not able to get it banned; all he was able to do was to get the casting-pen introduced. At that time, when a creature was driven into the slaughterhouse about six or seven men set on it and turned it upside down, stretched its neck back, the rabbi blessed it, and then its throat was cut. Well, this was a most terrifying thing for the animal and all that my husband was able to do was to get a law passed stipulating that the animal would be driven into a pen, and the pen would slowly revolve. I mean, that's ghastly enough, but it's not so terrifying as six or seven humans dashing at the animal.

In ritual slaughter, the animal is still forced to bleed to death.

Oh yes, it's a very, very cruel method. Mind you, when Moses brought this in, there weren't Humane Killers, there weren't means of killing animals humanely, and it was a health law in a hot country. It was at the time more humane to kill animals in that manner than to cut off odd limbs.

And of course animal flesh wasn't eaten so often in antiquity as it is today. It was only eaten at seasonal and religious festivals.

Possibly not. But I don't think it was ever meant to be a religious law; I think it was purely a health law.

I understand that there are movements afoot on the part of Jewish vegetarians to abolish ritual slaughter.

Well, I hope they're successful, because one of the things my husband did say in the House of Lords—and this was when he was speaking on vivisection—was that there is a law of cause and effect. In the Christian religion it is expressed in the adage "As you sow, you will reap," and in the Eastern religions it's called the law of karma. And he pointed out that we would never know true peace, health, or happiness while we brought terror, suffering, misery, and pain to all the younger forms of life.

What was the reaction when you and he founded Beauty Without Cruelty in the summer of 1960?

Oh, we were considered cranks and everything else. But the furriers know better. They have begun to take us very seriously, and they are putting up quite a fight. One of the biggest furriers in London, Swears and Wells, has closed, and its seventy-six branches are closing.

The "gin" trap has been outlawed in England and Scotland. When the bill was passed through, it was described as a diabolical instrument of torture. But we still manufacture them here for export— that's the hypocrisy of it! The gin trap is still being used in Canada and other countries.

Would you say that the gin trap is the most inhumane of the traps?

No. I think one of the most inhumane, if not *the* most inhumane method, is the way that they sometimes kill the big cats: they drive a red-hot poker up their rectum. You see, you must not mar the skin.

The Conibear trap, which is supposed to be less inhumane than the leg-hold traps, is seldom if ever used, because it is slightly more expensive than the leg-holds.

It's more expensive, and it's more difficult to operate. Personally, I don't think that you are going to be able to get a humane trap, really. It's a contradiction. You have to make up your mind that furs are cruel; there's no such thing as a humane fur. I mean, why should we take the skin of an animal? And of course leather—leather is very cruel.

But leather is a by-product of the slaughterhouse, isn't it? It's taken from an animal who has already been butchered for food.

Skin always comes off better from a live animal than a dead one. So reptiles are skinned alive. Little kids furnish the softest, most expensive leather.

Apparently, the scarcer the skin, the more attractive it is.

Oh, yes, but what Beauty Without Cruelty tries to do, and I think it's beginning—but just beginning—to succeed, is to make an animal fur not a status symbol, as it was perhaps twenty years ago, but a garment of shame. It was a great moment for me when I was in a train going North and I had on one of these simulated furs, and a rather nicely dressed, young woman sitting beside me said, "You look very nice, but I do hope your fur isn't real." I felt so elated to hear her say that!

There are so many groups and so many people now, particularly among the young. Women of 50 or 60 may cling to their furs (although quite a few are selling them) but I think that the young will not be so keen to have them; they won't view them as status symbols.

I think most vegetarians are, or become, a little more sensitive. Of course, today many vegetarians become vegetarians purely for health reasons. I was of a generation that didn't even realize that a vegetarian diet was healthy, but I wasn't going to have animals killed for me to eat. I became a vegetarian when my first husband was killed. I'd long had thoughts on this subject, but it was during the war, and the Vegetarian Society didn't seem to advertise itself very much. I didn't even know there was one. I had little idea what vegetarians ate, but when my first husband was killed, I thought, "Well, I always felt that I didn't want to eat animals, and now I'm definitely not going to."

It was many years after that when I felt that I had to do something about furs, and the last thing I *ever* thought of doing was founding a society. All I was going to do was try, with two friends, to put on a big London fashion show with someone to explain the cruelty behind furs and to show an alternative. At the end of this fashion show, which incidentally was packed—there had been a lot of publicity about it, because twenty years ago it was rather strange for a peeress to be staging a fashion show that promoted the wearing of fake furs because she felt real fur to be cruel—we were asked to take the show to fourteen of the main towns in England, which we did. Then people started to write to me, and my husband had to hire first one secretary and then another secretary. It was three years before we became a registered charity because I didn't want to form a society.

When did you first realize that beauty products were contaminated with animal ingredients?

Quite by chance I found out about the cruelty behind cosmetics. I had been married to my second husband about ten years when I started Beauty Without Cruelty. I knew about the cruelty of the killing of the whales—how explosive harpoons are shot into them and explode inside them, blowing up their intestines, and the frightful agony they die in—and at that time whale oil was used in many soaps, so I started to inquire about a soap that didn't contain it. In the course of my inquiry, I found out all the other animal ingredients in the soap.

In trying to find out about the soap—I always say that the angels are with us—through an extraordinary coincidence, I was put in touch with a very remarkable man in the trade, and it was largely through him that I learned one of the most closely guarded secrets of the cosmetic world. I learned not only the cruelty of the ingredients used, but the cruelty of the way they test the ingredients on animals. Shampoo is tested in rabbits' eyes. For testing dyes, they strip the skin from the back of an animal and rub various dyes onto the exposed nerves of its raw flesh. One of the most horrible tests is force-feeding lipsticks to an animal until its guts burst—I mean, no woman is going to sit at her dressing table and eat lipsticks!

Just as farmers raise battery hens, isn't it true that mink ranchers are now raising battery minks, for their furs and by-products?

Indeed, and foxes.

Are the conditions similar to those in the broiler house?

Yes. It was Dr. Harry Lillie who first told me of the cruelty in furs. He lived with the trappers and went round with them. He made a film called *Trapline*—a very good documentary, though rather old-fashioned now.

I said to him one day—and remember he is a Doctor—"I suppose if a woman is determined to wear fur, it is better that she should wear ranch fur rather than trapped."

His reply was, "If you were given the choice, Muriel, between a life of freedom terminated by a cruel and very horrible death, and a life spent in a cage with a quicker death—and remember animals are creatures of the wild; to them the sun, the wind, the rain and freedom is their life—which would you choose?

Well, it is a choice that the animal is not given. For myself, I think I might even choose to be wild and free and have the horrible death, rather than have no life at all.

Aside from mink products, is it true that even the most commonplace cosmetics— such as lipsticks, soap, skin cremes, perfumes—contain animal ingredients?

Yes, particularly the expensive perfumes, they use civet and musk.

Is it more expensive to use animal fixatives, rather than non-animal fixatives, in perfumes?

Yes, it is more expensive to use the animal fixatives, but it isn't as though there were no alternatives. For instance, for civet, which is the most widely used of the animal fixatives, there are something like eighty synthetic alternatives. In fact, the most expensive perfume in the world, *Joy,* has no animal fixative. A natural fixative that we use in perfumes is attar of roses.

Is ambergris from whales still a basic ingredient of perfumes and lipsticks?

Yes. You see, America has been very good about the whale. In England we are not so good. America, on the other hand, is of course abominable on the score of vivisection; it is appalling.

I understand that horses are kept in a state of perpetual foal and their urine is used in cosmetics.

Yes. Paddy Milligan (a Beauty Without Cruelty representative) once visited a pregnant mare farm in Canada and watched this being done. The urine of a pregnant mare yields estrogen, which is an ingredient of many cosmetics. Now, I mean, really, what woman wants to put that on her face?

Even domestic pets are used for soap-making.

Yes. That is not cruel, but it's not very nice. After all, a vet can't bury all the animals in his garden. Most vets have their practice in a town, and you can't have crematoria for animals in the middle of a town. So the animals are collected and transported to factories where the bodies—not in a very fresh condition—are melted down. Naturally, you have to add a powerful disinfectant and deodorant to all of this. And this is the basis of some soaps, cosmetics, lipsticks. Most people don't know that soaps and cosmetics contain these ingredients, you see.

Do the pores of the skin absorb these animal substances?

Well, I sometimes wonder. Many beauticians say, "Don't ever wash your face with soap!" I've always suspected that the animal contents, the animal ingredients, may be the basis for this caution.

Do you think that people are aware of the cruelty that precedes the wearing of a mink coat or an animal-tainted cosmetic?

Well, I would say that in this country, within the last few years, they have had an opportunity to learn about the cruelty behind cosmetics, because Baroness Phillips brought a bill in the House of Lords asking that animals should not be used for such a frivolous purpose as testing cosmetics. So that has very much opened up this possibility. We have an office that is absolutely swamped the whole time with requests for cruelty-free cosmetics. But I would say that, until two years ago, the general public didn't really understand. I would also think that certainly in this country few women are not aware that there is cruelty in fur.

How do the English aristocracy react to such an organization as Beauty Without Cruelty?

Some of them belong to it—not the vast majority—but some do. We get a good deal of support from the theatrical world.

I remember my husband coming home from the House of Lords and saying that a certain Peeress had come up to him and said, "I hate your wife."

My husband, who is very dignified, replied, "Madam, I was not aware you knew my wife."

The Peeress's reply was, "Oh, I don't, but I no longer like my mink coat!"

Do you think that the eating of animal flesh and the wearing of animal skins and furs are symbols of social status?

I'm not sure whether they still are. They certainly *were*.

Being able to wear fur, particularly ermine, was once, like flesh-eating, the pre-rogative of the nobility and the rich.

Oh yes, coronation robes and that sort of thing. You don't see much ermine about at the moment. It's nearly all mink. I was at a function not long ago. We sat down and a woman came in wearing a leopard coat. She sat just in front of us. My companion nudged me: "It's real!" And a man walked up to this woman, and said "Madame, is your coat real?" With much fluttering of the eyelashes, she said, "Oh yes." And in a very loud voice he said, "You should be ashamed of yourself!" Well, then the program started, but I was interested to see that when the lights went up for the interval, the coat was all rolled inside–out and hidden under her chair. Now, that is the sort of thing that will happen.

That's progress, isn't it?

Well, it is progress. I don't say that it happens every five minutes, but there is a growing consensus, especially among the young, that it is wrong to eat and wear animals.

Do you feel that before the world can become vegetarian, the various nations' leaders will have to set the tone?

No, I don't think that at all. My husband, who was incredibly wise, said, "Reforms don't come from governments. They don't come from the top. They come from people pushing from the bottom." The abolishing of the gin trap is one example: it wasn't a humane government that said, "We ought to abolish this." It was the people.

Who led them?

Well, you have to get a peer to introduce the bill into the House of Lords or someone in the Commons, but it was the pressure of the people. It didn't matter whether they were members of the aristocracy or what you perhaps would call the working class; it was the numbers that pushed, and pushed, and pushed. Oh, no, it's not going to come from the top. I think it will come from the bottom; the majority will be so overwhelming that film stars and what you would call "aristocrats" who wear furs will simply find that they are *so* unfashionable. And it will no longer be popular to wear them.

From time out of mind, people have endowed animal foods and animal substances with magical, prestige-enhancing powers. Do you think that may be one of the reasons why they are used in cosmetics?

No, it's because they're cheap!

I thought you said that they were more expensive than the nonanimal essences, scents, and fixatives.

No, no! We were just talking about perfumes. For Beauty Without Cruelty cosmetics, we use the best California avocados, almonds, and myrrh, you know, frankincense and myrrh, and how precious it is. We use these very lovely ingredients. Well, if you're going to go out shopping and buy some myrrh and some avocados and some almonds and cucumbers and all sorts of things that we use in our cosmetics, it will be much more expensive than if you were to go to a slaughterhouse and ask, "Have you got some nonedible fats that I can boil down? Have you got a few dead cats and dogs that I can boil down? What's the price of whale's ambergris, mink, crushed snails?" or whatever. Now, if you bring back that kind of witches' brew, it'll only cost you a few pence.

I understand that in the 1960s you went around to the cosmetics manufacturers and pleaded with them to stop using animal ingredients.

Well, I did go to several firms and ask them to make a range of cosmetics that did not involve any cruelty.

This was before you had established your own line?

Oh, yes. We should never have done it otherwise. I mean, it's been a nightmare to get our own products on the market because, you see, we were a very new organization: we hadn't any money at the back of us; we hadn't legacies and things. We only ventured it because the cosmetic firms refused to do it.

What was it that decided you to start your own line?

Partly because we did have on my council a very lovely woman named Kathleen Long. And she said, "Well, before my marriage, I was a chemist. I can make a range of cosmetics. During the War, I made them for friends, as they were in short supply, and because I don't like the muck that is put in the average cosmetic. In fact I do make my own, but," she said, "I couldn't do it from my back kitchen or anything like that, because if you're going to manufacture cosmetics, you must have proper conditions and be insured." And so from Kathleen's formula we got our first creme. A very big chemist in London made it up. It cost us 125 pounds to get the first batch on the market and from the little profit we realized from the first batch, we got the next one on the market. We've always kept our prices down, so that we're what is called mid-price. And we have built up now to a full cosmetic range.

Are you the only cruelty-free cosmetics manufacturer in the field?

There are other firms. Theirs is a very small range, however. I think we are the only people that do a full range. But we do publish a little booklet that we call *More Than Skin Deep* which itemizes all the beauty products of all the firms that have not been tested on an animal and do not contain any animal ingredient other than beeswax, honey or lanolin. Lanolin is from the sheep's wool after shearing; it's really sweat.

Do you think that wearing woolens is cruel?

Well, vegans don't wear woolens. I think there's exploitations in everything, but I don't think that wool is basically cruel, because I remember I had two pet lambs as a child and we had to get the local farmer in to shear them for their own cleanliness and comfort.

Do you envisage a day when everyone will use only animal free cosmetics?

Oh, I think it will come.

Are you gratified with the results that your organization has achieved in this field?

I'm very aware of our progress, yes, which I can measure by the number of branches of our organization that are springing up. So many people are writing and say, "I live in such-and-such place; could I start up a group here?" I mean, we don't say, "Will you start a branch?" They write to us. So many, in fact, write to us that we have to have a large secretarial staff to deal with all the enquiries.

I think one of the most notable things is that animals are now news. Twenty years ago they weren't. Practically every paper prints animal stories now.

Do you agree with the Indians that human souls may be embodied in animals?

I don't go quite so far as the Indians do because they won't put an animal out of its misery, will they? What I feel is that at the present moment man is the greatest destroyer this earth has ever known, and of course he will pay for it, and is paying for it, and will go on paying for it. But he is really meant to be the guardian and the teacher of all the younger forms of life, not their destroyer, which is what he is. He is at war with all the other forms of life. He pollutes the water; he poisons the earth with his chemicals—always for money.

Do you think that the vegetarianism that is starting to spread throughout the world will usher in a new Golden Age?

I do. Not long ago I had to read the lesson in Coventry Cathedral. And when I got there, I said, "Nobody's told me what I'm going to read." And they pointed to a pulpit very high up and said, "Well, it's in that great big book up there." Anyway, everyone was rushing around, much too busy with their own affairs, and I still didn't know when it was time for me to give the reading. My knees were knocking together—because I hate doing these sorts of things—as I went up there. And just then I had a premonition—a personal revelation, if you will—that the new Golden Age will come, because in that great big book, what had been chosen for me to read that day was a prophecy. It was the prophecy that the lion will lie down with the lamb.

    Now, that has actually happened, because there was a vegetarian lioness called Little Tyke who would never touch any form of flesh at all. She lived on grains, fruits, eggs, milk. She was absolutely beautiful, and they used her in films. Long, long ago, I saw her in a film. You could put any animal next to her. There is a picture of her on the cover of the book that was written about her life, called *Little Tyke,* with the lamb between her paws. Well, she was a prototype, a forerunner, for what the prophet was saying: "The lion will lie down with the lamb."

    The text goes on to prophesy various things of this nature, and it finishes up: "Because they will not hurt nor destroy in all my holy kingdom, because the world shall be so full of the knowledge of the Lord as the waters cover the sea." Now that was the prophecy of Isaiah. And we have left the Piscean Age, which has brought the love-teaching of Jesus. If you look at the end of the Piscean age, you will see that there is hardly an illness or an injustice that there aren't groups of people trying to help reform, and set right. I mean, look at all the animal welfare movements for instance.

We are now in the birth pangs of the Aquarian Age. The Aquarian Age is the age that should bring brotherhood between man and man, nation and nation, and between man and the animals. But I don't think we're going to see that until we come to the end of the Aquarian Age. We shan't live to see it. At least I shan't—you might. After all, we're only about fifty years into the Aquarian Age, and an age lasts over two thousand years.

Do you think that carnivorous animals may evolve into vegetarians, as did Little Tyke?

Oh, I think they will. I think the carnivorous animal can become vegetarian. I've had vegetarian dogs. Lions, dogs and cats have very short intestines: food passes through them very quickly. But they don't live very long, whereas vegetarian animals, like the elephant, ox and horse, have lovely sweet breath, and they live to be really a great age. As the carnivorous animals become vegetarian, I think their entire digestive apparatus will adapt.

Do you think man is a vegetarian by nature?

Of course he is. By nature, he should be a strict vegetarian, but I think he has been indoctrinated practically from birth with the idea that he must have meat. Many, many children, of course, don't want to eat meat, but then their mother or their nurse or someone tells them, "Oh, you won't grow to be a strong boy if you don't eat it." They're indoctrinated in that way. They're really forced to eat it willy-nilly. In my day, if you didn't eat your dinner up, when tea-time came, there wasn't a nice cake for you and dinner was put in front of you again. Children used to be brought up very strictly in England, and they had to eat what they were bade to eat. This may be changing nowadays.

Do you see other signs of progress?

Our present Prime Minister has said that he wants to reduce the number of animals used in experiments. Mr. Desai, the Prime Minister of India, has banned the export from his country of monkeys, reptiles, and other creatures. Mr. Desai is a vegetarian. Now here you have two Prime Ministers working for what my husband and I were working for.

You just do what you can, and then when you go, the next generation carries on. I mean, I'm standing on the shoulders of Nina Duchess of Hamilton and Miss Lind-af-Hageby and the people who fought for the animals in the previous generation. Their period of life on earth is gone, but people carry on their work. As I said, my husband and I stood on their shoulders, but there are lots who will stand on our shoulders.

Dick Gregory

In his two autobiographies, *Nigger* and *Up from Nigger,* Dick Gregory's favorite metaphors are drawn from track. Ever since he first discovered that he could outrun and outwit bullies in the black ghetto of St. Louis where he was born on Columbus Day, 1932, he has never stopped running—or polishing his celebrated wit.

In 1968, he embarked on his most ambitious marathon when he entered the race for the presidency. Unfortunately, his election results were not all they might have been. No doubt he would have made a better showing had Treasury agents not seized his campaign handbills, which had been printed in the form of dollar bills bearing a portrait of Gregory instead of Washington. (The T-men claimed they had been turning up in dollar-bill-changing machines, prompting Gregory to remark: "It's a heck of a commentary on technological advance, if a money-changing machine can't tell the difference between my face and George Washington's. I can't see how my face on a bill could confuse any human being or machine until the portrait of a black man appears on regular United States currency.") Not to be denied, he was proclaimed President-in-Exile by his supporters—an office which he held until August of 1974, when he relinquished it to his successor, Richard Nixon.

His humor always has had a social purpose. In the early 1960s he scored his first triumph as a comedian at the Chicago Playboy Club, satirizing race relations before an audience of frozen-food executives from the deep South. He is America's most conscience-stricken comedian. This is why, despite the barbed social commentary that he delivers to college-lecture and nightclub audiences, he is popular with crowds of all political colorations: beneath the japes and gibes, they sense the earnestness of a Gandhi in motley.

Although he made his debut before the public as a comedian in the early 1960s, he has since developed into something of a Renaissance man. He's become a talented author, whose sheer output other writers might envy: two autobiographies, a book of Bible tales, over half a dozen books on history and politics, as well as a book on nutrition, *Dick Gregory's Natural Diet for Folks Who Eat: Cookin' with Mother Nature*.

A few years ago, the comedian turned nutritionist came out with "Dick Gregory's Safe-Slim Bahamian Diet"—a diet nostrum that is made from a vegetarian powdered food supplement of his own devising that he calls "the 4X formula". Mixed with fruit juice, it supplies a nutritionally balanced meal. Not only has it made Gregory a millionaire many times over (the company moves millions of cans a year at $19.95 per can)—but it has also proved remarkably effective in reducing body fat in the chronically obese as well as in people who are moderately corpulent. Obese once himself (Gregory at one time tipped the scales at 288 pounds),—in the fall of 1988, he launched a national anti-obesity campaign, dubbing obesity America's number one nutrition-related problem. "America is the most obese nation in our world. We are 40 million tons overweight. Current estimates predict you lose at least one year of life for every ten pounds of excess body fat."

How long have you been a vegetarian?

Since 1965. Because of the civil rights movement, I decided I couldn't be thoroughly nonviolent and participate in the destruction of animals for my dinner. I didn't become a vegetarian for health reasons; I became a vegetarian strictly for moral reasons. As a matter of fact, when I became a vegetarian, I doubt if I had ever heard the word four times, and I'd never used it. I just said, "I'm going to give up meat."

Before I gave up meat, I never weighed more than 130 pounds. After I gave up meat and became a vegetarian, my weight went up to 288 pounds. It was because of fear: by not knowing how healthy it was, I really thought I was endangering my life. But I was willing to make that sacrifice from a moral standpoint. So I ate everything that wasn't an animal product. I was even drinking, smoking four packs of cigarettes a day. I didn't know about sugar or cholesterol. Anything that didn't have to be killed, I ate.

It was very interesting at that time in America. When you'd walk into a restaurant and tell the waiters that you didn't eat meat or fish, they'd really feel sorry for you so they'd bring out plates overloaded with vegetables. They thought that if you weren't eating meat, you wouldn't be healthy.

Then, also in America, the main course has always been the meat or the fish, and the vegetable has always been called the "side order." So it was in my head that I would have to survive on these side orders. Out of fear I ate as many of them as I could.

Then a funny thing happened: about 18 months later, my sinus trouble left, and about 6 months after that my ulcers disappeared. All this time I was still drinking and smoking. Had I quit drinking and smoking, I would have thought it was giving up cigarettes and alcohol that had cured me. I'd had sinus trouble and stomach problems since I was a kid. When these disappeared, I had no doubt that it was because I'd given up animal products. Then for the first time I realized that there might be more to food than I had ever thought. So I decided I would start investigating it. I discovered health food stores. Since I was making money, it was no problem for me to go into the health food stores and buy all the books. So after I had read widely in the literature, I started learning what true vegetarianism is all about.

How was it that you began to fast?

I started fasting the same way I got into vegetarianism—without knowing anything about it. When I used to read in the Bible that they would go into the wilderness and fast from food and drink, I thought that "food and drink" meant hot dogs, cheeseburgers, Pepsi and Coca-cola. Then it dawned on me that they didn't have all that stuff. When they fasted, that was it!

Do you think that fasting to further a political or moral cause is effective?

You fast to create a positive energy which can combine with all the positive forces. And it's that energy which has a tremendous effect upon society.

Now, in every good piece of literature on fasting that I read, it said that a public fast is a violation; to fast *for* something is in conflict with the universal order. I can understand that, because fasting is so powerful, so spiritual, and so beautiful. But I choose to use it as a public demonstration, because in America it has so much effect, mainly because of the way Americans feel about food. These people may not like your cause, but when they sit down to dinner, they think about your not eating, and they have to think about your cause.

I took up fasting as a protest against the war. I lived for 43 days on water and went from 280 to 95 pounds. One reason why I lost so much weight is because I was traveling, making speeches every night.

Fasting didn't diminish your energy or vitality?

No, my energy and vitality increased. When you abstain from eating for twenty-four hours, the energy that normally goes to digest food is released. Each day that you go without eating, you get stronger and stronger, until you become attuned to the harmony of the universe. Because our diets have been so bad, we've never felt that energy before and it seems as if we've acquired supernatural powers.

What do you think has been your most successful fast?

It's difficult to rank them like that. When I was protesting the war in Vietnam, I went for two years without eating solid food; I was just drinking fruit juice, I got so small that people would say, "Wow! I'll sure be glad when the war's over so he can eat!" I was getting letters from entire grade schools. A kindergarten whose children couldn't even write would draw a picture. Or you could see that the kids copied what the teacher wrote on the board: "Please Mr. Gregory, *eat!* The world needs you! God bless you!" And all their papers would be collected and mailed to me. That shows you the effect it had.

Not long ago I sent President Carter a telegram, explaining to him that I felt the investigation into the Kennedy-King assassinations to be one of the most important domestic issues. Before his inauguration I decided I was going to abstain from eating all solid foods until the investigation was reopened. I got a letter from him asking me not to fast, but it said that he understood. He never mentions the Kennedy-King investigation.

Now the effect of this is as follows: If I have to go four years without eating, I'll probably be so small that millions of people, particularly black folks, will start saying, "Dick Gregory is not going to eat until the Carter administration investigates the assassinations," and then they'll say, "I'll sure be glad when his four years is over so Dick Gregory can eat. If we put him in for four more years, Dick Gregory is going to shrink!"

So it's a magnet for publicity—a very potent force.

Yes, but also I think a fast can be a very powerful force even if nobody knows.

Christmas of 1975, I sent out a public notice appealing to anyone who wanted to dramatize the world food crisis by fasting. About 150 people came down to Atlanta and fasted from Christmas to New Year's. It was frightening, the power that was in that room. This was a strict water fast. There wasn't anyone on fruit juice. I don't think I would ever, ever again bring that many people together into a room and fast. I mean, that power was so strong, you could almost hear it.

Have you accomplished what you've set out to do through your fasts?

It's very difficult to say, because there are so many other people out working for the same cause. How many other people were bringing pressure to end the Vietnamese War? Mine may have been a small contribution, but I know that every bit of it was positive. I had a group of nuns and priests come to me. They said, "Dick Gregory, we've decided that we're so distressed by the war in Vietnam that we're going to fast until the war is over or until we die." I said, "Listen, you all had better go talk to the Pentagon about that. The Pentagon deals in death. I deal in life." So they changed their minds.

Is your family vegetarian as well?

Yes, my whole family is vegetarian. Ten of my eleven kids fast one day a week, and there hasn't been so much as one runny nose among them.

Have you influenced members of the black community to become vegetarians?

I would say that I'm probably one of the biggest influences in America today on both blacks and whites, mainly because of my college appearances. And in every book I write, I always mention something about vegetarianism.

Are a lot of black people becoming vegetarians now?

Oh yes, it's just unbelievable, unbelievable. A friend of mine who has a health food store in the black community; if she did under $4,000 a week, that would be a bad week. That's come after been out there for twenty years and barely surviving. I talked to a friend of mine in St. Louis who gives colonic irrigations—you know I recommend colonics in my diet book. He says that black folks come in there so fast to get colonics that now if he has a $3,000 week, then that's a bad week.

That's a very impressive statistic. But there isn't very much publicized in the media that black people are becoming vegetarians in such numbers.

Well, nothing is very much publicized in the media pertaining to black folks.

But that just goes to show how powerful vegetarianism must be. I'll tell you what really opened up this thing. Muhammed Ali and I are very close. He ran with me from Chicago to Washington, and then we ran from L.A. to New York last year. And for that last fight, I went up and stayed with him at his camp for ten weeks. A lot of information came out in those articles in *The New York Times* about the various things I had him on. That really, really turned a lot of black folks.

Have you managed to wean him from meat?

No, I never tried. You see, I didn't want to go to the Heavyweight Champ of the World and take him off meat. Let's say he might have decisively lost the fight; that would have been the worst detriment to vegetarianism. Because the press would have said, "Had he not become a vegetarian, he would have won the fight." Mothers and fathers would never ever have considered vegetarianism for their kids. It would have gotten world-wide negative publicity.

Do you think cancer is caused by meat-eating?

Sure, that's a known fact. It's no accident that the highest meat-eating nations have the highest incidence of cancer. And the highest beef-eating nations have the highest incidence of cancer of the colon and cancer of the bowel.

Do you know if hard evidence exists?

Yes. I mean, even the government knows that. The Russians did a good job on it. But even here in America, a lot of information has come out. One of the best studies is the government research of a group of Seventh-Day Adventists in California. Over a five-year period they found out that they had about 98 percent less cancer than the rest of the people in America, about 80 percent less heart disease. For every major disease we have, theirs is almost point zero.

During one of your celebrated fasts, didn't a doctor try to obtain a court order to force-feed you meat?

That was while I was in jail, fasting.

Another doctor said that fasting had created a superabundance of alcohol in your body, that your fast should be forcibly ended because you were too giddy to know what you were doing. How did this affect your opinion of the medical profession?

Someday I think the doctors will become dieticians; dieticians, doctors.

Do you think there are some enlightened physicians?

It's a small percentage, but I find a lot of doctors now who are more willing to consider diet and nutrition than ever before. But I think the people will lead the way. Once the people lead the way, then all the doctors and the medical schools will follow.

Shouldn't it be the other way around?

Well, the politicians didn't lead the way out of Vietnam, the people did. Vegetarianism will definitely become a people's movement. What with the crop blights, the droughts, the adverse weather patterns, and the high price of meat, the Vegetarian Society is going to win millions of converts just out of default. Why, look at the millions of people who don't eat as much meat now as they used to.

Perhaps with the famines throughout the world, it's become the humane thing to do.

They're not giving up meat because it's humane, they're giving it up because they can't afford it!

In your book, Dick Gregory's Natural Diet, *you jested about Colonel Saunders, the southern-fried chicken franchiser, that if he goes to heaven he may be ushered into the presence of "Chicken Big." Then you said you had visions of traveling to another planet where humans might be served as food. Does this imply that you think we will ultimately have to answer to a Supreme Being for our exploitation of animals?*

I think we answer for that every time we go to the hospital with cancer and other diseases.

So there's retribution in this world for eating animals?

Yes, there's a punishment for all negative action.

Are you an ethical vegetarian?

I don't know how ethical I am. I still wear leather shoes, and there's a bigger price on the hide than there is on the meat. I've never bought an $80 steak, but I buy shoes now that cost $110. The first thing I tried to do was to eliminate the killing of animals for my dinner. I buy as little leather as I can, but substitute leather shoes are very difficult to find.

What is the ideal food in your opinion?

The diet that comes closest to being perfect is fruit; it is the highest form of vegetarianism. By fruit I mean anything that has a seed in it. So that a lot of what we call vegetables are actually fruit, like tomatoes, cucumbers, squash, eggplant, bell peppers—they're really fruit.

Why do you emphasize fruit?

Because it comes closest to body chemistry: your body is 97 percent liquid against 3 percent solid, and fruit tends to have more water in it than anything else.

I've heard meat-eaters argue that plants have feelings, so that to slice a vegetable is no less reprehensible than killing an animal. How do you feel about it?

There's a difference between eating a pear and eating a pear tree: when a fruit ripens, it will fall off the tree and die anyway. If you don't harvest corn or lettuce, it will rot.

Do you find that you have to eat a quota of protein, a minimum dose, every day?

My thinking is this: If a steak is so good for you, because it has protein in it, where does the cow get its protein? There's no protein in grass. So I know that if I put the right minerals in my body, it will manufacture everything it needs. I don't have to eat finger-nails and toe-nails to grow finger-nails and toenails; I don't have to eat hair to grow hair.

I read that you ran 900 miles, taking only a kelp-based liquid formula as nourishment.

It was a formula called "4-X." It had about 17 different ingredients; kelp was the major ingredient. This formula could feed about 2 billion people a day, 3 meals a day, for 32¢, at a manufactured cost of a nickel.

In Dick Gregory's Natural Diet *you point out that more Americans die from overeating than from undereating. At the same time, you say that only about one American in ten escapes malnutrition. That seems paradoxical.*

Well, did you ever see a photograph of a kid with malnutrition? They have a bloated belly and a bald head, right? So go out to the airport and watch the executives come through the gates with their bloated bellies and bald heads—that's malnutrition too. Most people believe that malnutrition comes from not eating enough, but malnutrition can also result from eating the wrong combination of foods, or the wrong foods that are plentiful.

How do you account for the fact that life expectancy is relatively low in a vegetarian country like India, whereas a nation of beef-eaters such as the United States has a higher life expectancy?

Man, I went to India and saw so many old folks that it was scary. Whenever you have poor, poverty-stricken folks, you have a tremendous infant death. When they balance that against the adult mortality rate, it lowers life expectancy. It depends on how the figures are being juggled. Let me put it this way. Because of the abysmal poverty and lack of sanitary conditions which contribute to high infant mortality, if the life expectancy in India were twenty years, and if they weren't vegetarians, they probably wouldn't make eleven. Whatever the life expectancy is of a nation in which most of the people are vegetarians, I would say that it's still higher than it would have been if they were meat-eaters.

Many meat-eaters like to point to India as a bad example, an object lesson of what can happen to a country where most of the people are vegetarian.

India is a nuclear power; it has an army that is massed on the Chinese border, which prevents the Chinese from invading. I know that India produces enough grain each year to feed every Indian in India and export to the U.S., Canada, Russia, and China. But the problem is: 60–65 percent of their grain is consumed by rats and rodents. And that's what few people ever talk about. India is not overpopulated with humans, it's overpopulated with rats.

In your Natural Diet *book you point out that in the antebellum South, the master and his family lived on the choicest cuts of meat whereas the slaves, drawing on their African heritage, lived on organic fruits and vegetables, with only an occasional sliver of meat. Do you think they were healthier than the master by virtue of this diet?*

In many respects they were—physically, mentally. They had to be strong to withstand slavery.

Do you think this diet, consisting largely of organic vegetables, helped the slaves to survive?

That, and of course, the fresh air: they were outside, close to nature.

In your own childhood, you say that there was always a pot of vegetables brewing on the stove and that meat was a Sunday luxury. Would you sat that your diet was healthier than the diet of the rich folks?

It was healthier, but we weren't doing without meat because we wanted to. It was because we had to. We couldn't afford meat or else we would have eaten just as much as they did.

In both your Natural Diet *book and in* The Shadow That Scares Me, *you compare the ghetto with the slaughterhouse. Just as the rich are comfortably removed from the carnage of the slaughterhouse, they are insulated from the misery of the slum dwellers. Do you feel that the mistreatment of poor people bears a close relation to the mistreatment of animals?*

Yes, but from a different standpoint. If the super-rich who create the suffering and impoverished conditions in which the poor live could see what they are doing, they probably wouldn't do it. If most people had to go to the slaughterhouse and butcher their own hogs and chickens, they probably couldn't do it.

Do you think the lot of poor people will improve as we cease to slaughter animals?

I think so, yes. I would say that the treatment of animals has something to do with the treatment of people. The Europeans have always regarded their slaves and the people they have colonialized as animals.

Do you think that heavy meat-eaters are more prone to commit acts of violence than vegetarians?

I would think so, knowing how violent I used to be as a meat-eater.

Do you have any scientific evidence for this?

Just from myself and my vegetarian friends.

Do you think racial relations can be improved if we revert to what you feel is our proper diet?

I don't think you can limit it to that. Through proper diet, we can eliminate hostility and ill-feelings. All human relations would improve, and in the process racial relations would also improve. Through proper diet, marital relations, family relations, *all* relations will benefit.

Swami Satchidananda

Satchidananda was born in Coimbatore, South India, on December 22, 1914, the son of a wealthy landowner. Initially, he led a conventional life: marrying, having two sons, and building a career in the Indian automobile and motion picture industries. Upon the death of his wife in 1943, however, he renounced the world and became a mendicant *sadhu*.

In 1947, he joined the staff of Swami Bikku Swamigal, an itinerant monk who had been a naturopathic doctor before renouncing the world. Satchidananda helped the Swami to operate a traveling dispensary that worked remarkable cures among the "untouchables"—the lowest and most despised caste—by means of mud-packs, invigorating baths, herbal tonics and fasts. Their ministrations to untouchables were accomplished at great personal risk: often higher caste hindus would take offense and harass them, even threatening them with physical violence. In 1949, Satchidananda journeyed to the Himalayas where he met his guru—the venerable Swami Sivananda—from whom he received *sanyas* (initiation), and his name, "Satchidananda," which means "existence-knowledge-bliss absolute."

In 1953, Satchidananda established a branch of his guru's Divine Life Society in Ceylon and soon acquired a reputation for magnanimity and wisdom that spread far beyond the geographic confines of Ceylon. Conrad Rooks, a wealthy young American, flew to Ceylon in order to obtain film footage of Satchidananda that became a part of Rook's autobiographical movie of the late 1960s, "Chappaqua." After the filming, Rooks arranged for Satchidananda to tour Europe and the United States. Satchidananda created such a sensation in New York and attracted so many followers that he was persuaded to stay on and bring his teachings to the West, in the manner of Swami Vivekananda, Krishnamurti, and Paramahansa Yogananda.

His devotees purchased a lease on a shabby but serviceable nine room apartment on West End Ave. and 84th St. that functioned as the first Integral Yoga Institute. Since then, of course, the Integral Yoga Institute has multiplied; there is a branch in every major city in the United States. When he is not lecturing throughout the world at yoga institutes, universities, churches, rehabilitation centers, and vegetarian congresses—or writing (he has written a best-selling book on yoga asanas, *Integral Yoga Hatha*)—Swami Satchidananda divides his time between his ashrams, Yogaville East, in Pomfret, Connecticut, and Yogaville West, in Santa Barbara, California.

How long have you been a vegetarian?

From birth I have never tasted meat.

How many generations of vegetarians have there been in your family?

Countless generations.

The film-maker who persuaded you to come to America, was he already a vegetarian when he met you?

Yes; when we met he was just beginning his vegetarianism. Before that he had been taking all sorts of drugs: psychedelic, hallucinatory drugs.

It's interesting that so many yoga enthusiasts and vegetarians have emerged from the drug culture of the sixties.

I will give you a simple analogy. Who would be more likely to seek the shade, the people who dwell in darkness, or the people who have exposed themselves to the scorching rays of the sun?

Until yoga became widely accessible to Westerners in the 1960s there was no such technique for achieving self-deliverance and self-revelation as do the Hindu yoga adepts through vegetarian dieting, the asanas, and meditation. Perhaps, by taking these mind-expanding drugs—the hallucinogens, the psychedelics—they were seeking a sort of yogic self-deliverance via drugs.

Yes, but the real seeking begins only after you have exposed yourself to adversity; that is why you call adversities "blessings in disguise."

Sita Wiener writes in Swami *that for many years you subsisted on a diet of fruit and milk. Did you find that sustaining?*

Yes. I got into a sort of mono-diet because I believe that every natural food is well-balanced by itself. I don't have any research data to prove this, but common sense will tell you that a cow eats only grass, yet it brings forth milk that contains all the nutrients; therefore you ought to be able to derive all your nourishment from one type of food.

So I practice the mono-diet, and I don't need to balance one food against another. What's more, it is far less complicating for the stomach also. For a time I was eating only mung beans soaked and sprouted. Also, for a number of months I lived on only three cups of milk a day. That was the only nourishment I took—I never even had any fruit—and I was feeling so light, it was as if I were flying, cloud-walking.

Meat-eaters would contend that such a diet contains insufficient protein.

The meat-eaters get a lot of protein, no doubt, but it is an unclean protein. Furthermore, it is a highly complex, highly concentrated protein, and our system doesn't need that concentrated protein. It is not a question of how much protein you consume, but how much you assimilate that is important. A vegetarian diet provides more than enough protein in an easily assimilable form. The amount of protein that occurs in vegetables may not seem like a great deal when compared with meat, but you don't need that much. There has been an overemphasis on protein in western diet. Carrots, soy beans, avocados, lentils, grains, all contain a clean and natural protein.

Did you feel that your mono-diet supplied you with enough protein?

Oh, yes. I was quite healthy. I never lost weight. I never felt weak. If you keep your body in good shape, your digestive system in good shape, the digestive system can convert one food into whatever the body needs. Having experimented with the mono-diet for a number of years, I believe in it very firmly.

Do you feel that vegetarianism is essential to the practice of yoga?

Well, I won't say that it is essential, but it is very, very conducive to the individual who is practicing yoga, so naturally we recommend it.

Do you feel that meat-eating, on the other hand, can interfere with the practice of yoga?

In a way, yes, because meat contains all kinds of toxins and it is an unclean food. Meat-eating is undesirable if the person is interested in physical and mental well-being, in securing tranquility for the body and mind. Meat can never give that tranquility, because it introduces foul and toxic elements into the body. That is why meat-eating animals smell so awfully bad: the foul matter that is left by the meat in their system gives out a terrible odor whereas proper vegetarians do not have this foul matter in their bodies and will never give out this vile smell.

I assume that you mean to include meat-eating males and females of the human species.

Of course, that is why so many cosmetic factories are doing such a thriving business now by producing deodorants.

I've heard that Indians can discern the scent of meat in westerners.

I think that is a little too sweeping, because not all Indians are strict vegetarians. There are now many meat-eating Indians in India.

I understand that it was the Indian princes, the members of the ksatriya (or warrior) caste, who were the first in India to become westernized and eat meat.

Not all, but many did, because they were the only ones who had the money and the ability to come to the West. When they came to the West, they would live in "high society," go to the parties, and learn all of the western vices. Meat-eating was dignified. At the same time, not all the maharajahs fell under this influence. For example, Mysore Maharajah was a strict vegetarian, a great philosopher—a saintly person, I should say. He had his own gatherings. Not all of them succumbed. Some of them were very saintly people.

Do you feel that meat is widely regarded as a status symbol?

Yes. It is a symbol of false status, based on ignorance.

Do you think the great mass of vegetarians in India are vegetarian out of conviction or because they cannot afford the luxury of meat?

It's out of conviction. The greatest religious teachers have always recommended a vegetarian diet because it is a diet that stills the mind as well as strengthening the body. They are unanimous in saying that a peaceful mind, a serene mind, is necessary to recognize the God within you. "Blessed are the pure in heart; they shall see God," the Bible says. And yoga strives to calm and pacify the mind so that the person can recognize the God within.

A vegetarian diet helps to create this mental serenity. When people eat flesh food, directly the mind becomes restless. Take, for example, the animals in the zoo: all the meat-eating animals, with maybe one or two exceptions, are generally all restless. You don't see any calmness in their eyes; they are ferocious. Whereas the animals that eat vegetable food, they are peaceful. And they are the most powerful. The elephant is the classic vegetarian. And our motive energy is measured in horsepower, not in lionpower. So it is a vegetarian energy that we are using.

Actually the lion is quite lethargic.

Yes, but if it is aroused, it becomes ferocious.

Perhaps that's why westerners are so hyperkinetic and hyperactive compared to Indians.

Yes, flesh foods are irritating to the system and promote hyper-activity, whereas vegetable foods are *sattvic;* that is, they are soothing to the system and promote tranquility.

It has often been remarked that India suffers from an excess of spirituality, Europe from an excess of worldliness and materialism. Do you think that these differences in outlook may have arisen from a difference in diet?

Your entire thinking and perceptions can be altered by diet. You are what you eat. The mind can be refined by a vegetarian diet, coarsened by a flesh diet. However, I should argue that it is not all too spiritual in India. In many cases there is a misinterpreted, a misguided spirituality: it is too fatalistic. When God does not provide them with everything that they desire, they blame their fate and their karma. But if you just lie down and expect God to feed you, He will not feed you. In the name of religion they became lazy. But you cannot call it a failing of the Indian people or of India, and you cannot blame it on the diet. One of India's great spiritual giants, Swami Vivekenanda, once said, "Close up all the temples. Keep your scriptures shelved somewhere. Get onto the football ground and play football. You think that you are *sattvic,* that you are tranquil, but you are lazy. They both look alike, *sattva* (tranquility) and laziness, but you need *rajas* or activity; now come on, get up and play football!"

Westerners, on the other hand, are hyperactive. Most of their actions appear to be based on selfishness and violence. For their own gain, they are ready to do anything. They think they are wasting their lives if they do not spend it amassing money. But, of the two, who is happier? Ultimately it is peace and contentment that we are all looking for. But with all the money, with all the fame, with all the power, is the West peaceful?

I have heard it argued, however, that if this nation were to become vegetarian, its people would become too passive. Do you think being vegetarian prevents people from, for example, having business acumen?

People will do *better* business. They will have a genuine sympathy with the customer. They won't think of exploiting the customer, but rather of serving the customer; so they will befriend the customer and attract more customers to their business. Who is the good businessman? The one who thinks of the customer. You must put yourself in the position of the buyers; think of your self as spending their money. Our own health food store is such an example. People come to shop there and they feel so much at home.

For as long as the caste system has been in existence; the vaisya *(merchant) caste, whose members have traditionally been strict vegetarians, has in fact produced very astute businessmen.*

That is correct. Mahatma Gandhi was a *vaisya*.

In regard to the caste system in general, it has always puzzled me that a class system in which one caste is forbidden to look at, touch, mingle, or marry with another could have grown out of a culture that pays so much homage to ahimsa *(non-violence).*

Actually, the caste system was not originally intended to be the way it now is. In the scriptures it says that caste is based on temperament, not heredity. Who is a *Brahmin?* The one who is interested in spiritual matters. In knowing the Brahma, the absolute God, he is called a *Brahmin.* The next type of temperament belongs to the *Ksatriya,* or warrior. He has the temperament or personality of the soldier or professional fighting man, and he puts himself at the service of the country or community as its protector. The next temperamental type is that of the *Vaisya* or businessman. Whoever possesses a business mentality is called a *Vaisya.* The fourth temperament is that of the *Sudra.* They haven't the aptitude for priestly tasks, nor do they have the temperament for protecting the community, or doing business; so their duty is to serve the other three castes. There are four temperaments, but one and the same person can possess the characteristics of each temperament at different times. When I sit in my shrine room and meditate, I become *Brahmin.* When I go to the market and sell my goods, I become a *Vaisya.* If I am head of a family, and if I take care of the family and protect it from intruders, I am acting in the capacity of a *Ksatriya.*

So it is temperamental rather than hereditary. But you know, people are inclined to follow their father's profession, much more so in the past than today. A *Brahmin*, or priest's son tended to carry on his father's work, as did the sons of the *Vaisyas*, the *Ksatriyas*, and the *Sudras*. Generally these occupations became frozen into a kind of hereditary fraternity, with a fraternal group called *Brahmin*, a fraternal group called *Vaisya*. That is how the caste system came to be.

Fortunately now these distinctions are eroding, and the main credit should go to Mahatma Gandhi.

My own observation has taught me that one of the fears that Westerners have about becoming vegetarian is completely groundless. They have this image fixed in their minds of an emaciated, vegetarian Indian, but the strict vegetarian Brahmins *whom I met in India were well-fleshed and uniformly well-fed.*

Of course it is not vegetarianism that created the poverty and the famine. You must remember that for a long, long time the Indian people have been living literally as slaves under the rule of foreign conquerors. They were never given the facilities for a proper education. Now, after the freedom, India can boast many great scientists and inventors. Nowadays you could even call it a sixth superpower.

What about physical differences? Do you think that the average Indian vegetarian is a healthier specimen than his meat-eating western counterpart?

Undoubtedly. He is free from many of the Western problems and complaints.

Is there much cancer in India?
There doesn't seem to be much there. I have rarely encountered a cancer case.

Do you think that cancer and other degenerative diseases might be the result of eating meat?

That is certainly one of the causes; it isn't the only cause, but it is one of the causes. It is very hard for me to accept that meat is a clean food, free from any disease-producing qualities. And I will give you the reason: The animals do not offer their bodies with love when they are killed for their flesh. Right before they are slaughtered, they are terror-stricken. Fear races through their bodies, charging the meat with all sorts of poisons and toxins. Just as when you are frightened your system is sprayed with adrenalin, so too the animals, before they are slaughtered, are convulsed with fear and their systems are splashed with adrenalin. When the meat is cut out of the carcass, it is already charged with fright and shot through with toxins and hormones.

Even if you take animals to be butchered at a remote slaughter house hundreds of miles away, I believe that all of the animals within a certain radius can sense that their fellow animals are being slaughtered, and they cry and they may moan because of it. That is why meat can never be a healthy food: it is pain-poisoned. Whereas vegetarian food is freely given. An apple tree, for example, gives up its fruit most willingly. When the tree is ready to give it to you, you don't even have to pluck it; at a mere touch, it comes to your hands. When the fruit is ripe, the tree will drop it at your feet. Can you expect a goat to drop its tongue at your feet like that?

Vegetarian food is offered to us with joy, with love; it is an offering. But the meat of animals is not an offering; it is a plundering, a robbing. So the vibrations that follow the food affect our minds also.

Do you think that humans are innately violent?

No, not by nature. Essentially, we are peaceloving creatures. Our physical constitution. is not made for violence. We don't have sharp, piercing teeth or claws for rending flesh. We are built like a vegetarian animal. Our tongue, teeth, eyes, even our intestines belong to a vegetarian. Carnivores have very short intestines, only 5 or 6 feet, whereas the intestines of man—like those of the vegetarian, herbivorous, and frugivorous animals—are comparatively long, over 22 feet. Because it takes the meat such a long time to travel through the length of the human intestines, it putrefies and dispenses toxins in the system; whereas meat passes through the short intestines of a carnivorous animal very quickly, and all the poisons are expelled.

Many western anthropologists and historians hold that the evolution of the human species began with meat-eating. Do you think that homo sapiens *originated as a hunter?*

It could be. But I do not think that man was originally a hunter; I think he was originally a vegetarian. If he hunted animals at all, I think that he hunted them in self-defense, to prevent them from coming to destroy his food. Perhaps by watching carnivorous animals prey upon the vegetarian animals, he learned to hunt them and eat their flesh. But bear in mind that all of the other animals eat their food raw. Only human beings eat their food cooked. Suppose we were not able to cook our food: how many people would be prepared to eat meat raw?

Is the doctrine of reincarnation the chief reason why Hindus abstain from eating animal flesh?

Well, in a way yes. It is not really the doctrine of reincarnation that has had this influence so much as it is the doctrine of karma which says that every effect has its cause; every reaction, its action. So when you cause injury or violence to a person or an animal, you must face the inescapable consequences. It is for this reason that the Hindus do not want their lives to be given up to any violence. Violence only begets or causes more violence. It returns upon itself; it boomerangs. It is for this reason too, that many have held that it is better to die than to kill another creature and live.

What happens when one interferes with the karma of another being? What punishment would one incur?

It is not for us to say. The karmic law is not like our human laws which are codified and written out. But one must pay the penalty for one's negative actions. That is certain and unavoidable; it could come in any form. The person who kills an animal might die and take the form of the animal that he slew and then in turn be slain. It is a chain reaction. But people don't seem to realize that this law of cause and effect is everywhere at work; it is unavoidable.

Do you think it's possible to observe this law too closely? I understand that the Jains believe that the smallest insects have souls and therefore refuse even to swat a fly.

Well, that is one small sect. It is not possible in these modern times to go to that extreme. We must strike a balance between violence and nonviolence.

Now, do you wear leather shoes?

Yes, I do wear them. I don't carry it to that extreme. But I don't normally use many leather things. I try to avoid wearing leather but it is very hard to find shoes made of leather from an animal that has died a natural death. So when I have to wear leather shoes, I pray for that animal who died for the sake of my shoe.

I'm curious about the Rig Veda. *The first four books of the Vedic hymns were actually manuals for priests officiating at animal sacrifices. How can Hinduism, which urges* ahimsa *(nonviolence) and vegetarianism upon its followers, regard these books as holy?*

Well, the Vedas talk about everything. Not all matters that it treats are holy. It is divided into sections that cover the entire lifespan and the various activities of life. One major section is devoted to the performance of rituals for personal enhancement. Another major section is devoted to the welfare of the community and it is more spiritual.

The higher parts of the Vedas do not recommend animal sacrifice, because this can never be done for the welfare of humanity. In fact, as you go through it, you will find that most of the rituals involving animal sacrifice are performed for selfish reasons. If, for example, a king wants a son or if he wants to win a battle, he will perform a ritual, offering an animal in sacrifice. The esoteric meaning of these animal sacrifices is to sacrifice our animal tendencies and raise to a high consciousness. But in the Bible, too, there are parts that call even for human sacrifice: for example, the Lord ordered Abraham to sacrifice his son. But this does not mean that God was a cannibal or that the whole Bible should be judged on the basis of its violent parts. God simply wanted to test the faith of Abraham.

It is mistaken to think that the entire Veda is purely spiritual. It is a little like atomic energy; some atomic energy is used constructively, some destructively.

Do you think that, with the growing interest in yoga and vegetarianism, we might be on the verge of another Golden Age?

Yes. This is what people call the Aquarian Age. There are good signs that we may slowly be entering this new age. I am very optimistic about the future.

Helen and Scott Nearing

Scott Nearing is in his mid-nineties; Helen Nearing is in her mid-seventies, yet both work their farm in a manner that would put younger people to shame. One of the things that fascinated people about Helen and Scott Nearing is that they voluntarily chose to turn their backs on modern American culture in order to take up the arduous life of wresting a living from the land. At one time, going back to the land was thought of as a social and economic come-down, but the Nearings, both middle class intellectuals (Scott was an economics professor at the University of Pennsylvania, Helen a concert violinist), gloried in their homestead.

Together, the Nearings have built by hand more than a score of stone buildings on their property. They raise their own food and swap blueberries for clothes and tools; they are 85 percent self-sufficient in food, and 100 percent in rent and fuel. They have so budgeted their time that they have been able to reduce their "bread labor" to four hours a day, six months a year. The rest of the time they are free to devote to their professional interests: Scott's to writing and social science; Helen's to music.

The Nearings have made homesteading not only intellectually respectable, but also intellectually fashionable, and they have demonstrated that the life of the mind is not incompatible with the life of the land. Scott has written more than fifty books in his lifetime, and together he and Helen have written countless articles and two best sellers, *Living the Good Life* and *The Maple Sugar Book.*

Revered as the gurus of the back-to-the-land movement, each year the Nearings welcome some 2500 visitors to their farm who come to see for themselves how it is done. Not content merely to fend for themselves, they also have given 100 of their 150 acres to young couples who were eager to homestead but lacked the money to get started.

Many of the causes that the Nearings have championed throughout their lives—such as pacifism, vegetarianism, doctorless self-healing (neither Helen nor Scott has seen a doctor for over fifty years), back-to-the-landism, and organic gardening—have been taken up by a burgeoning segment of the population who have adopted the "Good Life" books as Baedekers to a better life.

Scott, when did you become a vegetarian?

Scott: About 1917, during the war.
Helen: He became a pacifist, a socialist, a vegetarian, all at once.
Scott: Well, I had a twenty-odd volume set of Tolstoy's works, and I studied those a good deal. I think he probably had more influence on me than any other writer. I never met him, but I could have. Helen, by the way, was born into a vegetarian family.

So you are a life vegetarian.

Helen: I picked my parents!

I understand that Upton Sinclair was a neighbor of yours in Arden, Pennsylvania.

Scott: He lived in our house. He lived in it winters, and we lived in it summers.

Did either he or his book, The Jungle, *influence you in your becoming a vegetarian?*

Scott: The Jungle probably appeared in 1907, at a guess. I read that with great interest and assigned it to my economics classes and used it a lot; but what they described in *The Jungle* was not new to me because I had learned the butcher's trade.

So you wouldn't have been astonished by anything you had read in Upton Sinclair. Did he ever become a vegetarian?

Scott: He did it experimentally. He toyed with it for a while. He didn't do it for cultural or moral reasons. We talked to him about it, and he tried it, and when he got through trying that, he tried something else. Eclecticism.

I understand that in your youth you worked in a slaughterhouse.

Scott: That's right.

Do you find butchery a degrading profession?

Scott: It's a degrading profession, certainly. But I never felt particularly ashamed of it or degraded by it myself until I began to take things seriously and to think for myself because in the town where I grew up, everybody raised small animals for food and killed them as a matter of course. We did the same thing: we had chickens, and pigs, and turkeys, and geese, and ducks, and ate them just as you would eat anything.

Are you the only vegetarian among the Nearings and your Nearing relatives?

Helen: Yes, that counts grandchildren and great-grandchildren.
Scott: I don't think there has been a single other vegetarian among my family.

It seems strange that no one was inspired by your example.

Scott: No. You see, I've never been very popular in my own family.

I understand that your family derided your diet somewhat.

Scott: Oh, yes. We dined at a table decked out with cutglass and doilies and silver and all the trimmings, but I used a wooden bowl, a wooden spoon, and a pair of chopsticks. My first wife did not approve of this simple service. My boy sided with my wife, and I was more or less isolated.

Did you get the idea from Tolstoy of using a wooden bowl?

Scott: No, I don't know where I got the idea of a wooden bowl.
Helen: It certainly has caught on. We go from commune to commune and meet these young vegetarian kids—there are increasing numbers of them—and they all eat with chopsticks and wooden bowls.

Do you think that vegetarianism is gaining acceptance?

Scott: Definitely. A few years ago, if you were a lettuce-eater, you were looked down on. Nowadays, in more cases than one, you're respected.
Helen: People invariably say, "I eat very little meat—I don't really like it." So they're coming around to it. About ten or fifteen years ago, if you said you were a vegetarian, you had to explain yourself. Now there are so many people there is hardly a family in the U.S. who hasn't got some vegetarianism somewhere. I think it is the coming thing.
Scott: It is only within the last ten or twelve years that you could get on an airplane and say, "I am a vegetarian, and the person in charge wouldn't say, "Well, what does that mean?"
Helen: Now they even say to us, "Are you a vegan?" That's going pretty far!

Who are some of the illustrious vegetarians you have known in your life?

Helen: Bernard Shaw, Annie Besant, Krishnamurti . . .
Scott: Was Krishnamurti a vegetarian?
Helen: He never tasted meat. He was from a Brahmin family.

Many Brahmins have gone over to meat-eating.

Helen: Many have turned, but in his day it wasn't done. He's about eighty now.

Of course, not a few vegetarians have been pacifists: Shelley, Shaw, Tolstoy . . .

Helen: Yes, and Gandhi.

Scott: It was the First World War that gave us a nudge in this direction, not in the beginning of the War, but as the War progressed and it became more and more ruthless and without justification. The First World War claimed 13 million lives.

As you point out in your autobiography, Scott, your high school French teacher used to refer to Napoleon as "le boucher." So many of the terms for the abattoir and the battlefield are interchangeable.

Scott: What does butchery mean? It means deliberate killing. In the law this is murder: killing with malice aforethought is murder, and slaughter of course is deliberate killing. You're commended for it during a war. When Ralph Jackman, a member of the International Workers of the World, (I.W.W.), was sentenced to Leavenworth, he met a chap there who had served in the War and drawn a long prison term at Leavenworth. He asked the chap how it happened that he was there. "Well," he answered, "I killed fourteen Germans at the right time and got the Distinguished Service Medal, then I killed one at the wrong time and got life."

Helen: Of course you have to remember that the Roman soldiers were vegetarians, and the gladiators who fought in the arena were kept on a grain diet; so not all vegetarians are pacifists.

Do you think that meat-eating is a form of conspicuous consumption?

Scott: In Europe and Asia, only the well-to-do really had meat. The poor people got meat once a week or once a month or once a year. In that sense, meat was a status symbol.

Of course during the Middle Ages one of the principal activities was the raising of flocks and herds. If you raised cattle or sheep or any other animals, certainly the male calves would be killed and the older stock would be killed so that almost inevitably then meat eating became more than a status symbol; it became an aspect of pasturage.

You mention that most of the people who come to visit you at Harborside, are members of the upper, and upper middle classes, and not the working class. Why do you suppose the interest in vegetarianism and homesteading isn't percolating up from the working classes rather than filtering down from the upper classes?

Helen: Because they want to have, and to experience, what they haven't had. The kids who come to us have had everything. The proletarian kids want what the others already have had; they want the best, the most expensive, the most propagandized.

How does vegetarianism fare in a communist country like Russia which is supposedly governed by the proletariat?

Scott: There used to be Tolstoyan restaurants in Russia, which meant vegetarian; of course Tolstoy had a special influence there.

Does vegetarianism flourish behind the Iron Curtain?

Scott: No, but it was recognized.
Helen: I wouldn't know where to find a vegetarian restaurant in Moscow now or in Leningrad. There may be some, but we haven't been there in a while.

How did the proletarian people in Russia and other communist countries regard your vegetarian diet?

Helen: Oh they were quite detached from it. They thought it was very strange that we didn't drink, because they always wanted to toast us. Once we were in Hungary, in a little village, and they brought out their best; but their best was liquor, meat, fish, white bread, cookies, candies, and vodka.
Scott: They offered us one thing after another and we had to say, "No thank you, no thank you, no thank you, no thank you."

So you don't mind declining food that doesn't agree with you.

Helen: We did mind, because this was their best, but we simply wouldn't eat the stuff.

Then your principles do prevail.

Helen: Oh, they hold. We have said "No" to more hostesses, but this was the most painful because these were poor people, and this was their best, and yet we said "No."

Were they offended?

Helen: Well, they didn't like it very much.

You don't subscribe to the fair-weather vegetarianism that the author, Edward Carpenter, practised.

Scott: He was a very famous writer of the previous generation, and he said that he never carried his vegetarianism far enough to inconvenience a hostess.

Helen: We have inconvenienced many hostesses. And Scott thinks that we should stay at home. When a thing like that happens, then we think that we really shouldn't travel, we really shouldn't bother people. So we don't go out much.

As a frequent visitor to India and the Orient, how do you account for the spread of meat-eating among Hindus?

Helen: Envy of the West, and of the power, wealth, and money of the West. Many have traveled to the West and learned to eat meat.

Do you think they've drawn the false syllogism that Westerners are prosperous because they eat meat, or do you think that a flesh diet is in fact responsible for the prosperity of the West?

Scott: No. Abundant natural resources are responsible for the prosperity of the West.

Meat-eaters would claim that a vegetarian diet makes people phlegmatic and passive.

Helen: Let them come up to Maine and work with us—we'll show them! Two years ago, CBS came up to interview Scott on the energy crisis. Scott took them up to the woodpile and said, "Here's some wood, and here's a saw. Get to it. No energy crisis for us!" They puffed and snorted, but Scott outdid them. They were meat-eaters of course, and half Scott's age.

Scott: Well, I just wanted to illustrate to them that if they wanted to help solve the energy crisis, it was necessary to have the food that produces energy.

Is the average vegetarian Hindu healthier than the average Westerner?

Helen: No, because the Hindu diet is a vile diet. It's white rice and overcooked food and overspiced food. It's a dreadful diet. It's vegetarian, but it's inferior to the produce diet that Western vegetarians favor.

But do they thrive on it?

Helen: I don't know any snappily vigorous women who jump out of a car and run into a store and run back again. They're so languid. And the heat is terrific—it's a ghastly climate. I wouldn't live in India for anything—of course I wouldn't live in Florida or Southern California for anything either.

How do you respond to the argument that vegetarianism is no less inhumane than meat-eating since plants are forced to yield up their lives for us.

Helen: Plants are obviously less sentient than animals. There's clearly a distinction between a new-born baby lamb and a newly ripened tomato.

You have to respect life in all its grades and forms. Most people who eat meat wouldn't eat their own babies, so they already have made a distinction there. We make a distinction between animals, on the one hand, and plants and vegetables on the other. We do as little harm as possible, and as much good as possible, and we think it is a higher degree of harmlessness to eat a tomato instead of a baby lamb.

Do you wear articles of clothing fashioned from animals?

Scott: We have a lot of trouble with belts and things of that kind. It's very hard to get that kind of thing out of any textile.
Helen: We try not to, but now and then we fail. We try to be consistent, but no one can be thoroughly consistent. Scott doesn't kill flies, but when they get too much for me, I do.

Then you're somewhat Jainist in your sympathies.

Scott: Yes.

In Living the Good Life *you write about the exploitation of domestic animals. Do you think that the abolition of animal slavery will be the next benchmark in human social progress?*

Nearings: Possibly.

Is it one of the failings of organized religions in the West that they have made no provision for the spiritual and temporal welfare of animals?

Helen: It certainly is.
Scott: The Essenes were vegetarians, and Jesus was an Essene, but their teachings have been widely ignored and forgotten.
Helen: I was up at the Trapp Camp . . .

The Trapp Camp? Is that a religious retreat?

Helen: The Trapp family? *The Sound of Music.*
Scott: They're Roman Catholic, Austrian aristocrats.
Helen: I was at the Trapp Camp, sitting next to Maria Trapp at dinner. I passed up all the exotic meat dishes and she said, "You don't like our food." And I said that I didn't eat flesh. She responded that our Lord did and so I told her, "First of all, you don't know if He did or not. And I don't care if He did or not—I don't." She didn't like that at all.

I wonder if the Western churches will reform their teachings, and begin to take animal welfare into account.

Helen: They should if they want to practice what they preach.

I've heard that you refuse to keep animals on your farm, in the belief that to do so would be mutually enslaving.

Helen: That's right. We have neighbors who have to be home to feed their cows, to do this, to do that—all to take care of these animals. They have constantly to play nursemaid to their animals.

Do you think city-dwellers are equally enslaved to the animals whose hides they use and flesh they consume?

Helen: They sure are. They have to work hard in an office in order to earn the money to buy expensive meats and leathers.

Is your life easier, do you think, than it might be if you were not vegetarians?

Helen: It sure is.

Scott: We succeed in producing the basic necessities of life in less than four hours labor a day.

Do you see your farm as a paradigm for households of the future?

Scott: No. It's only a transition farm. Forest Farm is a homestead, and on that homestead we are producing a basic livelihood. Any group of people like us or a larger group, an intentional community, any group, could take a piece of land and make a living on it, as the monasteries of the Middle Ages proved. They had industry, they had agriculture, they carried on education, they had art work, and so on and so on. They were autonomous units.
Helen: But not everybody could do it, not everybody would want to.

It takes a great deal of dedication and perspiration.

Helen: Yes, and know-how.

Did you come to this experience with the necessary know-how?

Helen: Scott did.
Scott: I was born and brought up in a small Pennsylvania town where everyone had a garden, a horse and a cow, chickens, a pig, and that kind of thing. And people were generally quite skilled in the arts of small-scale agriculture.

The man who has to work from eight to twelve hours a day . . .

Scott: He only thinks he has to.
Helen: In order to purchase the fancy things he wants, yes.
Scott: If he wants a car and a yacht and a home in the city and a house in the country, then yes. The question is, what do you want to do? Do you want to show off to your neighbors? Then these things are important. On the other hand, if you are interested in simplifying your life, and want to spend your time doing the things that interest you— Helen, for instance, likes to spend her time in music; I spend my time in social science—then these luxuries and status symbols are superfluous.

You think then, that man spends a disproportionate amount of his time in pursuing riches?

Scott: Instead of spending his time pursuing riches, he should spend his time in enough bread labor [the labor by which you procure your daily bread] to enable him to do the things that are really important in his life.

One of the themes of Shaw's Back To Methuselah *is that, since people fail to live out their allotted life spans—which he feels ought to approximate Methuselah's—they don't have the leisure to cultivate their minds and their interests, and their culture atrophies. Do you think a vegetarian diet will help to restore our life spans and reinvigorate our culture?*

Scott: A simple vegetarian diet will enable people to get their necessary bread labor performed and be able to go on with their professional work. And their professional work, that's the real contribution. Eating meals and maintaining one's body is not a real contribution.

I've read that animals generally live to seven times their maturity span. A horse matures at age three and lives to about 21. People mature at about age 20 so they should live to be about 140.

Scott: Well, now, the Russians are having a very interesting time with geriatrics. They're building up a bank of information on older people and they have case histories of all the people who are over ninety years of age. They're asking, "Why do these people get older without deteriorating physically and mentally?" What they've noticed is that, for one thing, these older people never retire. Whatever they are, instead of retiring at age 65, which for many westerners is tantamount to a death sentence, they keep on with what they have been doing, even though it may be on a reduced scale or at a slower pace. Another conclusion that the Russians are reaching is that the organism as is, barring accident, should last from 150 to 250 years. Now they don't say that we are going to have that tomorrow in Russia, but these are the possibilities of the human organism.

Well, there are the Abkhasians of Soviet Georgia, whom one might call the Methuselahs of the Caucasus.

Scott: Sure. They had one man die there recently at 167, I believe.

What about their diet?

Scott: Their diet? Well, I know that in Soviet Georgia, where they have a lot of these older people, or among the Hunzas in the Himalayas, they usually have a vegetarian, or a largely vegetarian, diet. They avoid extremes of activity and they avoid poisons: anything that tears down rather than builds up. Alcohol is a poison, white bread is a poison, sugar is a poison, excessive labor is a poison. Well, I wouldn't say that excessive labor is a poison—that's putting it a little harshly— excessive labor is disadvantageous.

I understand that during the traditional American feast days—Sundays, Thanksgiving, and Christmas—on which Americans gorge themselves, you two make a point of fasting. Why do you choose to fast when everyone else feasts?

Scott: We do it as a protest.
Helen: People who are already overeating overeat even more, especially on feast days.

Do you think that the leading causes of death, heart disease and cancer, are causally related to meat-eating?

Helen: We really aren't qualified to answer that question. But I think that if I found that I had a creeping cancer, I would immediately go on a long fast, and then eat only raw food. I think that I would conquer it that way.

When you feel just a bit under the weather, what do you do?

Scott: As a rule, if you feel some sniffles in your nose, in twelve hours you can cure it, if, first, you stop eating and then stop working. In other words, stop straining your body.

The theory behind this is very simple. If you cut your finger, you cannot heal that cut. The body has to do the healing. Doctors can't heal it; they can keep it clean, they can protect it, but they can't heal it. The healing work of reuniting the arteries, and the muscular tissues, and the nerve tissue—that's all done by the body. If you cut your finger, immediately an internal team of experts goes to work on that place. As a rule, you can't even see it when they get through, they do such a nice job.

Why do you suppose doctors haven't supported the vegetarian movement?

Helen: Because it's to their advantage that people be sick! If everybody were like Scott and me, where would the doctors be?

Scott: During the latter part of the nineteenth century, there was much discussion of the whole question of the effect of an over-proteinized diet on public health.

And what was the upshot of this discussion?

Scott: Well, the vegetarian movement, among other things. Ellsworth Huntington and Irving Fisher first raised the question as to whether a highly proteinized diet was sound. Fisher, who was a professor at Yale, wrote a book called *National Vitality,* which was an argument for a low-protein diet.

You see, protein is a body-builder in the young, but it's an excitant. Therefore, in the long run it becomes a depressant. The secretions of your glands drive you, drive you, drive you, and you burn the candle at both ends until the candle disappears.

Then during the years when one is developing and maturing physically, should one have a high protein diet?

Helen: As much as vegetables give you.
Scott: You need enough protein to build your body.

And this you feel can be derived from vegetable sources.

Scott: Vegetable protein, sure.

In classical antiquity, many great thinkers looked back on a Golden Age in which humans were vegetarians; they lived in harmony with one another and with animals, and warfare was unknown. Do you think that the vegetarianism that is now starting to spread throughout the world will usher in a new Golden Age?

Scott: There is a conscious effort on the part of a very large number of people to improve the conditions of life, whether by the health of the body, or the conditions of the social environment, or a wiser use of the natural environment. The sociologists call this "meliorism"—making things better. Now, this is a very widespread feeling in the world at the present time, and it has had enormous influence. This consciousness of the possibility of improving the conditions of life is something new in the world.

So, perhaps there is a chance for recovering the Golden Age.

Scott: The Golden Age—that sounds kind of mystical. There will never come a time when things cannot be improved. Life is an experiment, and if one thing doesn't work, then you make another effort. But you go on making efforts, and each experience gives you a certain amount of education and a certain basis of experimentation, and you go on from there. You do not go back to the cave, though there are cycles of expansion and contraction building up and wearing down. These cycles are geologic, and sociological, cultural, and, of course, cosmic. *Helen:* And they all have their place in the whole of life, just as winter has its place in the seasons.

Rynn Berry, Jr. was born in Honolulu, Hawaii. He has been a vegetarian since his junior year in college where he stored vegetables in a small refrigerator in his dormitory and cooked them on a two-burner hotplate. Majoring in classical archaeology and European literature, Mr. Berry did his undergraduate and graduate work at the University of Pennsylvania. He currently lives in New York and includes cooking, cycling, and book collecting among his hobbies.

Famous Vegetarians and their Favorite Recipes

Lives and Lore from Buddha to the Beatles

RYNN BERRY
Illustrated by Glory Brightfield

This lively potpourri of biographical profiles and favorite recipes provides an informal history of important vegetarians from antiquity to the present day. Included are Pythagoras ("Nut Stuffed Cabbage Rolls"), Gautama the Buddha ("Curried Spinach"), Jesus Christ, Plutarch, Shelley ("Eggless French Toast"), Tolstoy ("Soup Printaniere"), Annie Besant, Gandhi, and George Bernard Shaw ("Savory Rice"). Recipes were culled from cookbooks left behind or from the notes of family members and housekeepers. Other recipes were gleaned or carefully recreated from historical accounts. On the contemporary scene, Paul and Linda McCartney, Cloris Leachman, Isaac Bashevis Singer, and many more contributed their favorites.

FAMOUS VEGETARIANS is a persuasive account of how some of the most revered and successful people in many cultures have thrived on a vegetarian diet. The more than 70 recipes include soups, grains and pastas, soyfood entrees, vegetable entrees (nearly two dozen), salads and sandwiches, breads, and desserts.

RYNN BERRY's collection of interviews, *The Vegetarians*, was recommended by *Library Journal* and *Bon Appetit* and was the subject of an essay in *Time*. A vegetarian since 1966, he lives in Brooklyn, N.Y.

$14.95p, ISBN 0-915572-68-0;
7 x 10, line drawings, notes, bibliography, COOKBOOKS

PYTHAGOREAN PUBLISHERS
P.O. Box 8174
JAF Station
New York, N.Y. 10116